AMERICAN VOICES FROM

The Cold War

AMERICAN VOICES FROM

The Cold War

Elizabeth Sirimarco

BENCHMARK BOOKS

MARSHALL CAVENDISH
NEW YORK

Benchmark Books
Marshall Cavendish
99 White Plains Road
Tarrytown, New York 10591-9001
www.marshallcavendish.com

Library of Congress Cataloging-in-Publication Data
Sirimarco, Elizabeth, 1966–
The Cold War / by Elizabeth Sirimarco.
p. cm.—(American voices from—)
Summary: Presents the history of the Cold War through excerpts from letters, newspaper articles, speeches, and songs dating from the period. Includes review questions. Includes bibliographical references and index.
ISBN 0-7614-1694-3
1. Cold War—Juvenile literature. 2. World politics—1945—-Juvenile literature. 3. United States—Foreign relations—Soviet Union. 4. Soviet Union—Foreign relations—United States—Juvenile literature. [1. Cold War—Sources. 2. World politics—1945–1989—Sources. 3. United States—Foreign relations—Soviet Union—Sources. 4. Soviet Union— Foreign relations—United States—Sources.] I. Title. II. Series.
D843.S527 2003   909.82'5—dc21
2003001933

Printed in China
1 3 5 6 4 2

Series design and composition by Anne Scatto / PIXEL PRESS
Photo Research by Linda Sykes Picture Research, Inc. Hilton Head, SC

The photographs in this book are used by permission and through the courtesy of:

White House Photo/Archive/Getty Images: cover
Kreusch/AP Wide World Photos: ii
Hulton Archive/Getty Images: viii, x, xi, xiv, xvii, 5, 7, 14, 21, 36, 38, 44, 57, 70, 85, 89, 91, 94 (both)
Topham/The Image Works: xx, 41, 119, 125
Allan Jackson/Archive/Getty Images: xxiii
AP/Wide World Photos: xxiv, 28, 47, 53, 63, 81, 99, 103, 115

Library of Congress: 17
Rykoff Collection/Corbis: 24
UPI/Corbis: 34
The Image Works: 50 (both), 78
Jason Laure/The Image Works: 60
Black Star: 74, 106
Bettmann/Corbis: 82
Stapleton Collection/Corbis: 109
Eisenhower Presidential Library, Abilene, KS: 122
Eric Green, Museum Civil Defense Art

ON THE COVER: Mikhail Gorbachev and Ronald Reagan at a summit meeting in Washington, D.C., 1987

ON THE TITLE PAGE: The Berlin Wall goes up.

Acknowledgments

The author thanks the following sources for allowing their works to be reprinted here.

"U.S. Will Mobilize Planes in Europe to Supply Berlin" copyright © 1948 *New York Times*. Reprinted with permission.

Excerpt from *The Berlin Candy Bomber* by Gail S. Halvorsen copyright © 1997 by Horizon Publishers and Distributors, Inc. Reprinted with permission.

Excerpt from *Thirteen Days: A Memoir of the Cuban Missile Crisis* by Robert F. Kennedy. Copyright © 1968 by McCall Corporation. Used with permission by W. W. Norton & Company, Inc.

"I-Feel-Like-I'm-Fixin'-To-Die Rag" copyright © 1965 by Tradition Music, BMI; renewed 1993 by Alkatraz Corner Music, BMI. All rights reserved.

"We Will All Go Together When We Go" copyright © 1958 by Tom Lehrer. Used with permission.

Samantha Smith's letter and the response from Yuri Andropov are reprinted here with permission of Mrs. Jane Smith.

"The Urgency of the Nuclear Threat," interview with Dr. Helen Caldicott. Reprinted with permission from John M. Whiteley, University of California, Irvine.

Excerpt from *Listening to America: Twenty-five Years in the Life of a Nation as Heard on National Public Radio,* edited by Linda Wertheimer. Copyright © 1995 by National Public Radio. Reprinted with permission of Houghton Mifflin Company. All rights reserved.

Extract from *The Camera Never Blinks Twice: The Further Adventures of a Television Journalist* by Dan Rather and Mickey Herskowitz. Copyright © 1994 by Dan Rather.

Contents

CAPACITY
1730

FALLOUT SHELTER

A primary source can be many things—a beloved photograph, a handwritten note, a poster—even this sign indicating the location of a fallout shelter.

About Primary Sources

What Is a Primary Source?

In the pages that follow, you will be hearing many different "voices" from an important period in America's past. Some of the selections are long while others are short. You'll find many easy to understand at first reading, but some may require several readings. All the selections have one thing in common, however. They are primary sources. This is the name historians give to the bits and pieces of information that make up the record of human existence. Primary sources are important to us because they are the very essence, the core material for all historical investigation. You can call them "history" itself.

Primary sources *are* evidence; they give historians the all-important clues they need to understand the past. Perhaps you have read a detective story in which a sleuth has to solve a mystery by piecing together bits of evidence he or she uncovers. The detective makes deductions, or educated guesses based on the evidence, and solves the mystery once all the deductions point in a certain direction.

Historians work in much the same way. Like detectives, historians analyze the data by careful reading and rereading. After much analysis, historians draw conclusions about an event, a person, or an entire era. Individual historians may analyze the same evidence and come to different conclusions. This is why there is often sharp disagreement about an event.

Primary sources are also called *documents*—a rather dry word to describe what can be just about anything: an official speech by a government leader, an old map, an act of Congress, a letter worn out from too much handling, an entry hastily scrawled in a diary, a detailed newspaper account of a tragic event, a funny or sad song, a colorful poster, a cartoon, a faded photograph, or someone's eloquent remembrance captured on tape or film.

By examining the following primary sources, you, the reader,

Albert Einstein
Old Grove Rd.
Nassau Point
Peconic, Long Island

August 2nd, 1939

F.D. Roosevelt,
President of the United States,
White House
Washington, D.C.

Sir:

Some recent work by E.Fermi and L. Szilard, which has been communicated to me in manuscript, leads me to expect that the element uranium may be turned into a new and important source of energy in the immediate future. Certain aspects of the situation which has arisen seem to call for watchfulness and, if necessary, quick action on the part of the Administration. I believe therefore that it is my duty to bring to your attention the following facts and recommendations:

In the course of the last four months it has been made probable - through the work of Joliot in France as well as Fermi and Szilard in America - that it may become possible to set up a nuclear chain reaction in a large mass of uranium,by which vast amounts of power and large quantities of new radium-like elements would be generated. Now it appears almost certain that this could be achieved in the immediate future.

This new phenomenon would also lead to the construction of bombs, and it is conceivable - though much less certain - that extremely powerful bombs of a new type may thus be constructed. A single bomb of this type, carried by boat and exploded in a port, might very well destroy the whole port together with some of the surrounding territory. However, such bombs might very well prove to be too heavy for transportation by air.

-2-

The United States has only very poor ores of uranium in moderate . . . . quantities. There is some good ore in Canada and the former Czechoslovakia, while the most important source of uranium is Belgian Congo.

In view of this situation you may think it desirable to have some permanent contact maintained between the Administration and the group of physicists working on chain reactions in America. One possible way of achieving this might be for you to entrust with this task a person who has your confidence and who could perhaps serve in an inofficial capacity. His task might comprise the following:

a) to approach Government Departments, keep them informed of the further development, and put forward recommendations for Government action, giving particular attention to the problem of securing a supply of uranium ore for the United States;

b) to speed up the experimental work, which is at present being carried on within the limits of the budgets of University laboratories, by providing funds, if such funds be required, through his contacts with private persons who are willing to make contributions for this cause, and perhaps also by obtaining the co-operation of industrial laboratories which have the necessary equipment.

I understand that Germany has actually stopped the sale of uranium from the Czechoslovakian mines which she has taken over. That she should have taken such early action might perhaps be understood on the ground that the son of the German Under-Secretary of State, von Weizsäcker, is attached to the Kaiser-Wilhelm-Institut in Berlin where some of the American work on uranium is now being repeated.

Yours very truly,
A. Einstein
(Albert Einstein)

A letter from Albert Einstein to President Franklin D. Roosevelt, warning that Germany may be capable of building an atomic bomb. The letter, an excellent example of a primary source, led the president to commission the Manhattan Project, a program charged with beating the Germans in the race to harness atomic energy.

will be taking on the role of historian. Here is a chance to immerse yourself in a fascinating era of American history— the Cold War. You will come to know the voices of men and women who lived through this harrowing period. You will read the words of politicians and ordinary citizens, intellectuals and activists, journalists and military leaders.

Some sources you will read may be difficult to understand at first. You may encounter some challenging words and concepts, or formal language. Don't be discouraged! Trying to figure out language is exactly the kind of work a historian does. Like a historian, when your work is done, you will have a deeper, more meaningful understanding of the past.

SUNDAY EXPRESS

Founded by LORD BEAVERBROOK

DECEMBER 29 1946

LIGHTING-UP TIME 4.28 p.m. to 7.39 a.m.

Moon D Rises 11.37 a.m., Sets 10.7 p.m.

TWO

Scientists of the secret U.S. atom bomb factory announce a—

REVOLUTIONARY ATOMIC DISCOVER

Power can be produced NOW almost as cheaply as by coo

Experts ready to build the power houses

OUR WHOLE ECONOMIC SYSTEM MAY BE CHANGED

by Gerald Johnson, Sunday Express Special Correspondent
New York, Saturday

THE NEWS STORY THAT, ON THE FACE OF IT, IS BY FAR THE BIGGEST OF THE YEAR IS THE PROGRESS REPORT OF "THE MANHATTAN PROJECT." THE ARMY ORGANISATION THAT DEVELOPED THE ATOMIC BOMB.

The story has been given out grudgingly and piecemeal, but apparently the Manhattan Project is now in the position to build installations that will convert atomic energy into electric power at a cost per unit only slightly in excess of the cost of producing such power from bituminous coal.

The military mind so resents the necessity of telling civilians anything that Major-General L. R. Groves, the Officer of Engineers at the head of the project, has given out only as much information as he deems necessary to counteract the rumours about his organisation.

These rumours were not nice. They described Groves as running a devil's smithy, in which he had 50,000 people at work forging weapons strong enough to destroy mankind.

Nobody really believed these yarns, but there was so much talk that Congress was threatening to order the general to come out in public and say what he has been doing. So, reluctantly, he permitted his Press agents to tell the main facts, without details

Part of it came out through Karl Compton, president of the Massachusetts Institute of Technology, part through Bradley Dewey, president of the American Chemical Society, and part through incidental Press releases prepared by anonymous Press agents.

Question of cost

The important part of the statement—the assertion

Former Minister of Justice accused

Murder charge

THREE well-dressed men were charged at West London yesterday with the murder of John McMain Mudie, the former Eighth Army corporal whose body was found in a chalk pit at Woldingham Common, Surrey.

The men, who were remanded in custody until next Friday, are :—

The Hon. Thomas John Ley, 66, of Beaufort-gardens, Chelsea, S.W., well-known City business man, solicitor of New South

Irgun say 'Will flog British officer'

As 'reprisal'

JERUSALEM, Saturday.—The Jewish terrorist organisation Irgun Zvai Leumi announced in pamphlets distributed to-night in Jerusalem and Tel-Aviv that a British Army officer would be flogged in retaliation for the flogging of Abraham Kimchin.

Kimchin was sentenced to a term of imprisonment with 18 strokes of the birch for his part in the Jaffa bank robbery on Sept. 13.—Reuter.

Met Terrorist No. 1

How did U.S. Congressman Bald-win, under the nose of the British police and Army in Palestine, meet Menahem Begin, No. 1 wanted Jewish terrorist in Palestine? He has a price of £2,000 on his head.

Did he in fact meet Begin, long believed to be in Paris, of some junior terrorist stooge? cables Sunday Express correspondent from Jerusalem.

These questions were being asked when news spread of a cabled appeal from the Congressman to the terrorist leader.

Stories about the actual meeting itself say that Mr. Baldwin saw Begin—or a junior terrorist—in darkness at a farmhouse near Tel-Aviv. He was accompanied by three hooded men.

Declaring he is reporting to President Truman and Congress, Mr. Baldwin stated :—

"I appeal to you to halt operations in the Holy Land, at least until I have had the opportunity to acquaint the American Government and people with your fight.

"Remember my assurance to you that I will do all in my power to present your point of

WHEN THE GATES CLOSED AT HIGHBURY

ON the outside—and not look-ing in. A section of the disappointed thousands at High-bury, yesterday, is in the picture above, taken when the "Gates closed" notices were posted.

That was half an hour before the kick-off in the Arsenal v. Wolves match. Sixty-three thousand managed to see the game of the year—it ended in one goal each—but between 10,000 and 15,000 fans were turned away

Hundreds waited around the entrances, throughout the game in the hope of gaining admission. Occasionally mounted police had to rush the crowd when attempts were made to break in.

Half an hour before the match the rush at Arsenal Underground station was great, and Ano-ther forms were jammed with the human tide up Highbury-hill.

Home-goers besieged the station, too. Gates were shut, as

platforms filled, and reopened, at intervals, as packed trains drew out. There was some doubt whether the cleared before the match would be ended. Police helped railway officials to keep order.

Thousands of private cars—hundreds of motor-coaches—many from the Midlands—lined all streets leading to the ground. Some enthusiasts managed to see the game by scrambling over fences and climbing to the top of nearby blitzed buildings.

New 'coal or we shut' warnings by factories

RAIL WAGON CRISIS

FROM all parts of the country last night there came reports of growing fears of further big industrial slow-downs owing to the coal situation.

Two factors dominate the situation — shortage of coal and inability of transport undertakings to deliver the approximate daily

DEADLY NEW 'FOOT AND MOUTH'

Cattle slaughte

The headlines of a 1946 British newspaper describe a "revolutionary discovery" by Manhattan Project scientists: electric power produced by atomic energy.

How to Read a Primary Source

Each document in this book deals with the Cold War. Some of the documents are from government archives such as the National Security Archives. Others are from the official papers of major figures in American history, such as President Harry S. Truman. Other documents are taken from the letters ordinary people wrote. All of the documents, major and minor, help us to understand what it was like to live during the Cold War.

As you read each document, ask yourself some basic but important questions. Who is writing? What is the writer's point of view? Who is the writer's audience? What is he or she trying to tell that audience? Is the message clearly expressed or is it implied, that is, stated indirectly? What words does the writer use to convey his or her message? Are the words emotion-filled or objective in tone? If you are looking at a photograph, examine it carefully, taking in all the details. Where do you think it was taken? What's happening in the foreground? In the background? Is it posed? Or is it an action shot? How can you tell? Who do you think took the picture? What is its purpose? These are questions that help you think critically about a document.

Some tools have been included with the documents to help you in your investigations. Unusual words have been defined near the selections, and thought-provoking questions follow each document. You'll probably come up with many questions of your own. That's great. The work of a historian always leads to many, many questions. Some can be answered, while others cannot and require more investigation. Perhaps when you finish this book, your questions will lead you to further explorations of the long, tense, troubled era that came to be known as the Cold War.

Russian revolutionary leader Vladimir Lenin (1870–1924). Lenin founded the radical group known as the Bolsheviks, which evolved into the Soviet Union's Communist Party.

Introduction

A DIFFERENT KIND OF WAR

When you begin to study the Cold War, there is something important to understand: it was not a war in the traditional sense of the word. This "war" raged for nearly fifty years between the Soviet Union and the United States and their respective allies, yet never did Americans and Soviets face each other in combat. During the Cold War, America's enemy was not a soldier dressed for battle. It was an idea—and, by extension, the people who believed in the idea. That idea was communism.

The divide between the Russians and the West—Europe and the United States—began with the Bolshevik Revolution in 1917. For three centuries the czars had ruled Russia; the ruling class lived lavishly while the poor suffered a grim and joyless existence working for the benefit of the wealthy. A radical group called the Bolsheviks (which means "majority") began to stir up discontent among the people. Led by Vladimir I. Lenin, the Bolsheviks touted the theories of Karl Marx, whose writings include the *Communist Manifesto*. Marx, a German economist and philosopher, formulated his theory of communism based on socialism, an economic system that emphasizes public or community ownership of farms, factories, and other means of production. Communism takes the idea of sharing ownership a step further, giving governments control of all property and resources.

Marx called for an end to capitalism, a system in which the chief means of production are privately owned. He said that capitalism concentrates wealth into the hands of a small portion of the people, who then use their economic power to control government and society. This system divides people into two groups, owners and workers, leading inevitably, Marx claimed, to poverty and injustice. He predicted that workers—or the proletariat—would grow dissatisfied with this unfair system, which benefits only the wealthy class. This discontent would lead to revolutions in which workers would take control of governments all over the world. They would then use socialism to dismantle capitalism, abolish private property, and create communist governments run by the proletariat. A country run by a communist government would result in a classless society with no individual wealth, and it was this ideal that inspired Lenin and the Bolsheviks to take action. On the night of November 6, 1917, they seized the Russian government, and the nation soon became known as the Union of Soviet Socialist Republics, or the Soviet Union.

Unfortunately, life under Lenin and his Communist Party, the political party created by Russia's new leaders, was no better than it had been under the czars. The proletariat was not trusted to play a role in the government. Instead, a powerful cadre of elite officials began to make all decisions for the nation. After Lenin's death, when Joseph Stalin came to power, things only became worse.

The Bolsheviks, shown here with other prosocialist leaders, seized the Russian government in November 1917. The nation would soon become known as the Soviet Union.

Stalin held a brutal grip on the Soviet people. His secret police ensured that there was complete loyalty to the government. Criticism was not tolerated; those who spoke against the government were liable to be imprisoned—or worse. During the 1930s Stalin sent between 17 million and 22 million people to their deaths for being "enemies of the state." Under communism, the Soviet Union became a totalitarian state, one in which there was no freedom of speech or freedom of the press, a nation in which the people had no individual rights whatsoever.

In addition, the practice of religion was seriously discouraged, because the Communists claimed that it "enslaved" the people. More importantly, they thought, the church took power away from the state. Although the Soviet government never actually outlawed religion, it did what it could to eliminate it. Church property was confiscated and atheism was taught in schools. Those who practiced religion were harassed and, because the government controlled the workplace, believers had little opportunity to advance in their careers. They were also forbidden to join the Communist Party.

The Soviet government was fundamentally different from the democracy of the United States, a country founded on principles of freedom. A capitalist nation, America embraced private ownership and the idea that anyone, with sufficient determination and hard work, could become prosperous and successful. That a government could take away this possibility seemed unthinkable. From its earliest days, the United States emphasized democratic ideals—from freedom of speech and religion to the right to a fair trial; any nation that denied its citizens such rights was viewed with suspicion and mistrust. While emphasizing the separation of church and state, Americans supported belief in God and the practice of religion, asserting that government simply should have no say in private matters. Overall, the United States—and the West in general—viewed communism as an immoral system and the Soviet Union as a godless country that suppressed the rights of its people to achieve the goals of its privileged leadership.

For its part, the Soviet Union believed the capitalist nations of the West exploited their working class. Eventually, the Soviet leaders predicted, communist revolutions would take place in those countries as well. There seemed to be no way to bridge the gap between the two ideologies. As the years passed, Americans and Western Europeans looked on with horror as the communist government took hold in Russia. There was little communication between the Soviet Union and the West. But when World War II erupted, everything changed—for a time.

War broke out with the German invasion of Poland in September 1939. At first, the Soviet Union surprised many by allying itself with Nazi Germany. But in June of 1941, after the German army invaded their nation, the Soviets joined with the United States, Great Britain, and the other Allied Powers. It was an uneasy alliance, born of the necessity to defeat the Nazis and burdened with the mutual distrust arising from the nations' very different ideologies.

In November of 1943 the Allies' Big Three wartime leaders—Winston Churchill of Great Britain, Franklin D. Roosevelt of the United States, and Joseph Stalin of the Soviet Union—met for the first time. Together they agreed to launch a massive offensive the following spring, much to the relief of the Soviets. For many months the Soviets had been bearing much of the weight of the struggle against Germany along the war's eastern front. Now the Western powers promised to open a second front. The following spring, millions of American, British, and Canadian troops would strike from the west. In turn, the Soviet Red Army would launch a simultaneous offensive from the east, virtually surrounding the Germans. On June 6, 1944—D-Day—Allied troops landed in Normandy, France, opening the second front as promised.

Over the next several months, it became apparent that the combined efforts of Soviet and Western forces would ultimately be

The Big Three: *(left to right)* Joseph Stalin, Franklin Roosevelt, and Winston Churchill. This photo was taken at their first meeting, held in Tehran (Iran) in 1943, when they agreed to launch a joint offensive against the Germans. The commitment would ultimately bring about the end of World War II.

successful. In February 1945 the three powers met again, this time in the Soviet city of Yalta, to determine the future of postwar Europe. Already signs of trouble between East and West could be seen. Stalin feared that the United States and Britain would attempt to dominate European affairs after the war. He was also concerned that they would control the United Nations, the newly formed international peacekeeping organization. Germany had occupied Poland during the war. Disputes arose about what kind of government it should have once the Germans were removed. Britain wanted to return Poland's former government to power. The Soviets wanted Poland—as well as other nations in Eastern Europe—to act as a buffer between the Soviet Union and Germany. They hoped to install a new pro-Soviet government for Poland. Roosevelt and Churchill feared that Stalin intended to push communism into Poland.

Though the war was drawing to a close in Europe—Germany would surrender in May—it showed no signs of doing so in Japan. The United States was anxious to enlist Soviet help in that conflict. Ultimately Britain and the United States agreed to Soviet dominance of Poland in exchange for its assistance in Japan. It would be a decision the United States would later regret, for soon the Soviets would establish a stronghold across Eastern Europe. In time the region would be run by communist governments, all of which answered to a higher power: the Soviet Union.

As the Yalta Conference came to a close, it was clear that only the mutual goal of defeating Nazi Germany had brought the three nations together, for the differences between East and West—between communism and capitalism—were vast. With the death of Franklin D. Roosevelt shortly after the meeting at Yalta, what trust had existed between the Soviets and the Western powers would soon erode.

A contributing problem to U.S.–Soviet relations was the devastation that Russia had suffered during the war. While some 300,000 American soldiers died in the war, an estimated 27 million Soviets had lost their lives—civilians and soldiers alike. The country was in desperate straits: war had devoured nearly one-third of its wealth. Factories lay in ruins, homes were gone, farms destroyed. Some 70,000 towns had been burned to the ground, and thousands of miles of railroad track were now useless. In contrast, the United States ended the war with great wealth, having earned billions of dollars manufacturing wartime munitions. In fact, it was now the greatest industrial power in history. Its economy had nearly doubled during the war. Capitalism—the most fundamental enemy of communism—was in full swing. Such extremes would lead to further division between East and West.

Nevertheless, as the war in Europe came to an end, Russian and American soldiers met for the first time. The troops had fought from different fronts, never shoulder to shoulder. On April 25, 1945, American troops approached Soviet Red Army units near the town of Strehla, Germany, firing green flares to signal that they were friends. As the soldiers came together, they embraced. With Russian vodka, they toasted Stalin, Roosevelt, and Churchill. Troops from both sides swore that they would do everything to ensure peace and friendship between the two nations. Two days later, more Americans and Russians came together, this time in Torgau, along Germany's Elbe River. Photographers from both

U.S. soldiers shake hands with Russian troops at Torgau, a town on the Elbe River, south of Berlin. Such optimistic camaraderie between Americans and Soviets would be short lived.

sides were there to capture the event, and people all over the world witnessed the historic moment. It seemed that a new era of peace was on the horizon.

Instead, the world was poised at the edge of a new conflict: the Cold War, a battle of ideologies that held the potential for more death and destruction than any "hot war" in history.

After Germany's surrender, the Allies divided Berlin, the German capital city, into four sectors, controlled respectively by the Soviet Union, the United States, Great Britain, and France. Here German women clear lingering wartime rubble along the boundary between the British and U.S. sectors.

Chapter I

From Ally to Enemy: The Cold War Begins

GERMANY OFFICIALLY SURRENDERED on May 7, 1945. The end of the conflict in Europe called for another meeting of the Big Three, but this time two of the players would change. Roosevelt died shortly after the Yalta Conference, and President Harry S. Truman now represented the United States. Churchill was in attendance early on at the new meeting, held in Potsdam, Germany, during July and August of 1945, but he was voted out of office before the conference ended. The new prime minister, Clement Attlee, would arrive to replace him. Only Stalin would last through both conferences.

In addition to officially dismantling the Nazi government, one of the main topics at Potsdam was how Germany would be governed. The Allies decided to divide it into four occupation zones, with the Soviets in the east and the United States, Great Britain, and France in the west. Berlin, the capital city, which lay deep within the Soviet-controlled zone, was divided up as well. The western part of the city, which would later come to be known as West Berlin, would be occupied by the United States, Great Britain, and France. The

Soviets would control the eastern sector of the city. In time, Berlin would become the first "battleground" of the Cold War.

The end of war in Japan brought about another event of great significance to the Cold War. On August 6, 1945, after delivering an ultimatum to the Japanese to surrender or face serious repercussions, the United States dropped the world's first atomic bomb on the city of Hiroshima. It exploded with tremendous force, and the heat and the blast were followed by 500-mile-an-hour winds. Much of the city was destroyed in a matter of minutes. At least 70,000 civilians were killed instantly, and thousands more would die from radiation poisoning in the months and years that followed. Three days later the United States dropped a second atomic bomb, on the city of Nagasaki, bringing an end to the war in the Pacific without an invasion. The swift Allied victory kept the Soviets, who on August 8 had declared war on Japan, from occupying any part of the island nation. Americans would have total control over postwar Japan.

With such an invincible weapon at its disposal, the United States gained tremendous power. Scrambling to catch up, Stalin funneled government money—funds desperately needed to rebuild his nation after the war—into a program to develop an equally potent weapon. The arms race had begun.

Although East and West had cooperated during World War II, it became clear soon after the war that the sharp contrasts between them had never disappeared. The Soviet Union was still a regime, run by a dictator, that denied freedom and democracy to its people. Already at Yalta Roosevelt had sensed reason for concern over Soviet policy in Poland and other Eastern European countries. Americans feared the Soviets intended to extend their communist principles—and their rule—to lands beyond their borders, perhaps ultimately throughout the world. This was not something the United States or its allies could allow.

Historians disagree as to the true start of the Cold War. Some say it began when Stalin gave a speech blaming World War II on capitalist nations. He also said that communism and capitalism could never coexist. Others consider Winston Churchill's famous "Iron Curtain" speech as the opening to the Cold War. In March 1946 Winston Churchill visited President Truman in the United States. Churchill told Truman of his concern that the Soviets were trying to control a growing expanse of Eastern Europe. Together they decided that Churchill should give a speech to alert the world to the Soviet threat. In that speech, Churchill used the term *Iron Curtain* for the first time. The term would come to symbolize the barrier between the West and the nations of Eastern Europe that were dominated by the Soviet Union. Still others believe the Cold War began when the United States offered help to Turkey and Greece, where communist guerrillas were fighting—with Soviet help—to overthrow their governments. Regardless of when the Cold War actually began, in the late 1940s U.S. officials determined it necessary to contain the spread of communism at all costs.

A President's Thoughts: Truman at Potsdam

After the death of Franklin Roosevelt on April 12, 1945, Harry Truman found himself thrust onto the world stage at a critical point in history. At the Potsdam Conference that summer, he met Churchill and Stalin for the first time. The night before the conference began, he learned that a major event had taken place back in the United States. Scientists had successfully tested the first atomic bomb. Since 1942 American and British scientists had been working to develop this weapon. The top-secret project was known as the Manhattan Project. Several days after the test, Truman received word that the bomb was even more powerful than expected. This weapon—a single bomb—had the power to destroy a city in minutes. Truman kept a diary while he was president. The entries that follow, written during the Potsdam Conference, offer insight into a period in U.S. history that would change the world forever.

JULY 16, 1945

Mr. Churchill called by phone last night and said he'd like to call [in person]—for me to set the hour. I did for 11 a.m. this morning. He was on time to the dot. His daughter told Gen. Vaughn he hadn't been up so early in ten years! I'd been up for four and one half hours. We had a most pleasant conversation. He is a most charming and very clever person. . . . He gave me a lot of hooey about how great my country is and how he loved Roosevelt and how he intended to love me etc. etc. I am sure we can get along fine if he doesn't try to give me too much soft soap. . . .

JULY 17, 1945

Just spent a couple of hours with Stalin. . . . Promptly a few minutes before twelve I looked up from the desk and there stood Stalin in the doorway. I got to my feet and advanced to meet him. He put out his hand and smiled. . . .

After the usual polite remarks we got down to business. I told Stalin that I am no diplomat but usually said yes and no to questions

after hearing all the argument. It pleased him. I asked him if he had the agenda for the meeting. He said he had and that he had some more questions to present. I told him to fire away. He did and it is dynamite—but I have some dynamite too which I am not exploding now. . . .

I can deal with Stalin. He is honest, but smart as hell. . . .

"The most terrible bomb in the history of the world"— ironically dubbed "Little Boy" by Manhattan Project scientists

"I can deal with Stalin."

JULY 25, 1945

We [Truman, Churchill, and Stalin] met at 11:00 a.m. today. But I had a most important session with Lord Mountbatten and General Marshall before that. We have discovered the most terrible bomb in the history of the world. . . . An experiment in the New Mexican desert was startling—to put it mildly. Thirteen pounds of the explosive caused the complete disintegration of a steel tower sixty feet high, created a crater six feet deep and twelve hundred feet in diameter, knocked over a steel tower a half mile away, and knocked men down ten thousand yards away. The explosion was visible for more than two hundred miles and audible for forty miles and more. . . .

It is certainly a good thing for the world that Hitler's crowd or Stalin's did not discover this atomic bomb. It seems to be the most terrible thing ever discovered, but it can be made the most useful.

—From the "President's Secretary Files," Harry S. Truman Papers, Harry S. Truman Library, Independence, Missouri.

THINK ABOUT THIS

1. What traits of character about himself do Truman's diary entries reveal?
2. What did Truman think of Stalin? Do you think his opinion of Stalin would change in the future?

The United States Bombs Hiroshima

President Truman had a difficult decision to make. U.S. leaders were certain the war in the Pacific could not end without an invasion of Japan. Such an offensive would require an estimated two million U.S. troops and would result in tremendous loss of American life. Truman and his aides recognized that the deadly atomic bomb could bring a swift and decisive end to the war. Following are highlights from the statement President Truman made to the American public after the bombing of Hiroshima on August 6, 1945.

SIXTEEN HOURS AGO AN AMERICAN AIRPLANE dropped one bomb on Hiroshima, an important Japanese Army base. That bomb had more power than 20,000 tons of T.N.T. It had more than two thousand

President Harry S. Truman was forced to make a difficult decision. To save American lives and end the war with Japan, he approved the use of the atomic bomb.

times the blast power of the British "Grand Slam" which is the largest bomb ever yet used in the history of warfare.

The Japanese began the war from the air at Pearl Harbor. They have been repaid many fold. And the end is not yet. With this bomb we have now added a new and revolutionary increase in destruction to supplement the growing power of our armed forces. In their present form these bombs are now in production and even more powerful forms are in development.

It is an atomic bomb. It is a harnessing of the basic power of the universe. The force from which the sun draws its power has been loosed against those who brought war to the Far East. . . .

The fact that we can release atomic energy ushers in a new era in man's understanding of nature's forces. Atomic energy may in the future supplement the power that now comes from coal, oil, and falling water. . . . Before that comes, there must be a long period of intensive research.

It has never been the habit of the scientists of this country or the policy of this Government to withhold from the world scientific knowledge. Normally, therefore, everything about the work with atomic energy would be made public.

But under present circumstances it is not intended to divulge the technical processes of production or all the military applications, pending further examination of possible methods of protecting us and the rest of the world from the danger of sudden destruction.

I shall recommend that the Congress of the United States consider promptly the establishment of an appropriate commission to control the production and use of atomic power within the United States. I shall give further consideration and make further recommendations to the Congress as to how atomic power can become a powerful and forceful influence towards the maintenance of world peace.

—From "Statement by the President of the United States, August 6, 1945."
To read the entire press release, visit the Truman Presidential Library website:
http://www.trumanlibrary.org/whistlestop/study_collections/bomb/small/mb10.htm

THINK ABOUT THIS

1. The bomb had the ability to end World War II, but are there other reasons Truman seemed pleased that the United States was the first to harness atomic energy?

2. How could the atomic bomb be a "forceful influence towards the maintenance of world peace"?

The Russian Situation: Kennan's Long Telegram

In February 1946 Stalin gave a speech to the Soviet people in which he denounced capitalism, claiming it was responsible for World War

II and would inevitably lead to future conflict. This pronouncement was of great concern to Western leaders. By drawing such a firm distinction between communism and capitalism, the speech seemed to signal Stalin's "declaration" of cold war. U.S. leaders sent an urgent request to George Kennan, an official at the U.S. embassy in Moscow, asking him to analyze Stalin's motives. In response Kennan sent an eight-thousand-word cable with his interpretation of the speech and a recommendation that the United States do everything possible to contain the spread of communism. Following are portions of that famous telegram, beginning with a summary of what Stalin had said. The language may seem choppy; when people wrote telegrams, they tried to use as few words as possible. They would drop anything that wasn't necessary to convey meaning.

SECRET

Moscow, February 22, 1946—9 p.m. . . .

KENNAN DESCRIBES THE SOVIET VIEW OF WORLD AFFAIRS—
- (a) USSR still lives in antagonistic "capitalist encirclement" with which in the long run there can be no permanent peaceful coexistence. . . .
- (b) Capitalist world is beset with internal conflicts. . . .
- (c) Internal conflicts of capitalism inevitably generate wars. . . .
- (d) Intervention against USSR, while it would be disastrous to those who undertook it, would cause renewed delay in progress of Soviet socialism and must therefore be forestalled at all costs. . . .
- (e) Conflicts between capitalist states, though likewise fraught with danger for USSR, nevertheless hold out great possibilities for advancement of socialist cause. . . .

KENNAN DESCRIBES SOVIET PLANS—

(a) To undermine general political and strategic potential of major Western powers. . . .

(b) . . . efforts will be made to weaken power and influence of Western Powers [on] colonial backward, or dependent peoples. . . .

(c) Where individual governments stand in path of Soviet purposes pressure will be brought for their removal from office. . . .

(d) In foreign countries Communists will, as a rule, work toward destruction of all forms of personal independence, economic, political, or moral. Their system can handle only individuals who have been brought into complete dependence on higher power. . . .

(e) Everything possible will be done to set major Western Powers against each other. Anti-British talk will be plugged among Americans, anti-American talk among British. Continentals, including Germans, will be taught to abhor both Anglo-Saxon powers. Where suspicions exist, they will be fanned; where not, ignited. . . .

(f) In general, all Soviet efforts on unofficial international plane will be negative and destructive in character. . . .

KENNAN OFFERS SUGGESTIONS FOR U.S. POLICY—

Gauged against Western world as a whole, Soviets are still by far the weaker force. Thus, their success will really depend on degree of cohesion, firmness and vigor which Western world can muster. . . .

(a) Our first step must be to apprehend . . . the nature of the movement with which we are dealing. We must study it with same courage, detachment, objectivity, and same determination not to be emotionally provoked or unseated by it, with which doctor studies unruly and unreasonable individual.

(b) We must see that our public is educated to realities of Russian situation. . . . I am convinced that there would be far less hysterical anti-Sovietism in our country today if realities of this situation were better understood by our people. . . .

(c) Much depends on health and vigor of our own society. World communism is like a malignant parasite which feeds only on diseased tissue. . . .

(d) We must formulate and put forward for other nations a much more positive and constructive picture of world we would like to see than we have put forward in past. . . .

(e) Finally we must have courage and self-confidence to cling to our own methods and conceptions of human society.

—From George Kennan, telegram to the Secretary of State, February 22, 1946. To read the full text of the "Long Telegram," visit the National Security Archive at George Washington University: http://www.gwu.edu/~nsarchiv/ coldwar/documents/episode-1/kennan.htm

THINK ABOUT THIS

1. In Kennan's view, did the Soviets believe that capitalist nations could win in a conflict with the Soviet Union?

2. According to Kennan, how did the Soviets plan to spread communism?

3. What are some ways that Kennan suggested the United States should oppose the Soviet policies? Do any of his ideas make sense for U.S. world policy today?

The Truman Doctrine: A U.S. President Wages Cold War

The speeches by Stalin and Churchill represented what many consider their countries' unofficial declarations of cold war. The U.S. declaration would follow in March of 1947. Communist rebels were striving to overthrow the governments of Greece and Turkey, and

Truman and his advisers believed the United States should support the existing governments. In a speech broadcast to the nation on March 12, he asked Congress to vote for economic aid to Greece and Turkey. Improving the economies of these nations would help prevent the spread of communism, he said. Truman also identified the threat of communism as a global one that applied not only to Greece and Turkey, but to all of Western Europe and Asia as well. Truman's speech set forth what became the U.S. policy to provide economic assistance to any nation threatened by communism, a policy that would be in effect throughout the Cold War. It became known as the Truman Doctrine.

ONE OF THE PRIMARY OBJECTIVES of the foreign policy of the United States is the creation of conditions in which we and other nations will be able to work out a way of life free from coercion. This was a fundamental issue in the war with Germany and Japan. Our victory was won over countries which sought to impose their will, and their way of life, upon other nations. . . .

At the present moment in world history nearly every nation must choose between alternative ways of life. The choice is too often not a free one.

One way of life is based upon the will of the majority, and is distinguished by free institutions, representative government, free elections, guarantees of individual liberty, freedom of speech and religion, and freedom from political oppression.

The second way of life is based upon the will of a minority forcibly imposed upon the majority. It relies upon terror and oppression, a controlled press and radio, fixed elections, and the suppression of personal freedoms.

I believe it must be the policy of the United States to support free peoples who are resisting attempted subjugations by armed minorities or by outside pressures. I believe that we must assist free peoples to work out their own destinies in their own way. I believe that our help should be primarily through economic and financial aid which is essential to economic stability and orderly political processes. . . .

"The seeds of totalitarian regimes are nurtured by misery and want."

The seeds of totalitarian regimes are nurtured by misery and want. They spread and grow in the evil soil of poverty and strife. They reach their full growth when the hope of the people for a better life has died. We must keep that hope alive. The free peoples of the world look to us for support in maintaining their freedoms. If we falter in our leadership, we may endanger the peace of the world—and we shall surely endanger the welfare of this Nation.

—From President Truman's speech to the nation, March 12, 1947. To read the speech in its entirety, visit http://www.trumanlibrary.org/trumanpapers/pppus/1947/index.htm

THINK ABOUT THIS

1. Truman said the world must choose between alternative ways of life. What are the two choices to which he referred, and how do they differ?
2. According to Truman, what factors promote the spread of communism?

Marshall Announces His Plan for European Recovery

In 1947 the U.S. secretary of state, George Marshall, traveled to the Soviet Union to attend a conference. While there, he spoke with Stalin and learned the Soviets were convinced that capitalism in

Europe was nearing its demise. The continent had yet to recover from the devastation of the war, and Stalin believed that widespread poverty and misery would cause many Europeans to look to communism for a solution. Upon his return to the United States, Marshall wasted no time. He set to the task of creating the European Recovery Program, which would become known as the Marshall Plan. He and his staff devised a way to create economic cooperation among European nations and to stimulate economic growth. He hoped that if conditions in Europe improved, communism would lose its appeal. The world first learned of the program in June 1947, when Marshall gave the commencement address to Harvard University graduates. A portion of that speech follows.

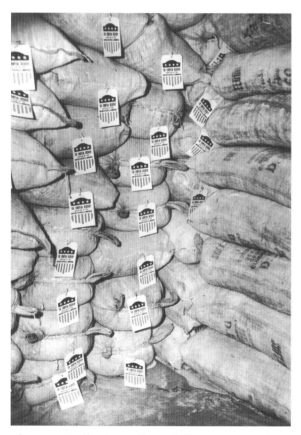

The Marshall Plan allowed for massive shipments of food to help Europe recover from the devastation of the war. The tags on these flour bags aimed for Austria read, "For European Recovery supplied by the U.S.A."

THE TRUTH OF THE MATTER is that Europe's requirements for the next three or four years of foreign food and other essential products—principally from America—are so much greater than her present ability to pay that she must have substantial additional help or face economic, social, and political deterioration of a very grave character. . . .

Our policy is directed not against any country or doctrine but against hunger, poverty, desperation, and chaos. Its purpose should be the revival of a working economy in the world so as to permit the emergence of political and social conditions in which free institutions can exist. Such assistance, I am convinced, must not be on a piecemeal basis as various crises develop. Any assistance that this Government may render in the future should provide a cure rather than a mere palliative. Any government that is willing to assist in the task of recovery will find full cooperation, I am sure, on the part of the United States Government. Any government which maneuvers to block the recovery of other countries cannot expect help from us. Furthermore, governments, political parties, or groups which seek to perpetuate human misery in order to profit therefrom politically or otherwise will encounter the opposition of the United States.

> *"Our policy is directed not against any country or doctrine but against hunger, poverty, desperation, and chaos."*

—*From Secretary of State George C. Marshall, commencement address at Harvard University, Cambridge, Massachusetts, June 5, 1947. To read the full text of this speech, visit the Web site of the George C. Marshall European Center for Security Studies: http://www.marshallcenter.org/*

THINK ABOUT THIS

1. What was the ultimate goal of the Marshall Plan?
2. Do you think Europeans might have turned to communism because of the economic difficulties they faced after the war?
3. Can you find phrases in Marshall's speech that might have been meant for the Soviets?

Chapter 2

The Arms Race

BY THE END OF 1947, the division of East and West was complete, and the Cold War had begun. The Soviet Union controlled nearly all of Eastern Europe; Western Europe was anxious to contain the further spread of communism. George Marshall, in hopes of keeping Western Europe free, urged Congress to approve his plan for economic aid. For his part, Stalin viewed the Marshall Plan as a U.S. attempt to control Europe. In addition, the plan would help Germany recover from the war, and the Soviets were not ready to see this happen. They believed Germany could still pose a serious military threat. They also wanted the Germans to suffer for the devastation they had caused. Regardless of Stalin's motives for refusing to commit to the Marshall Plan, the United States saw his opposition as an act of aggression, and tensions escalated further.

While Congress was debating the Marshall Plan, which would be a very expensive undertaking, another Eastern European country fell to the Communists. In February 1948 Communists took control of the government of Czechoslovakia, and fear struck

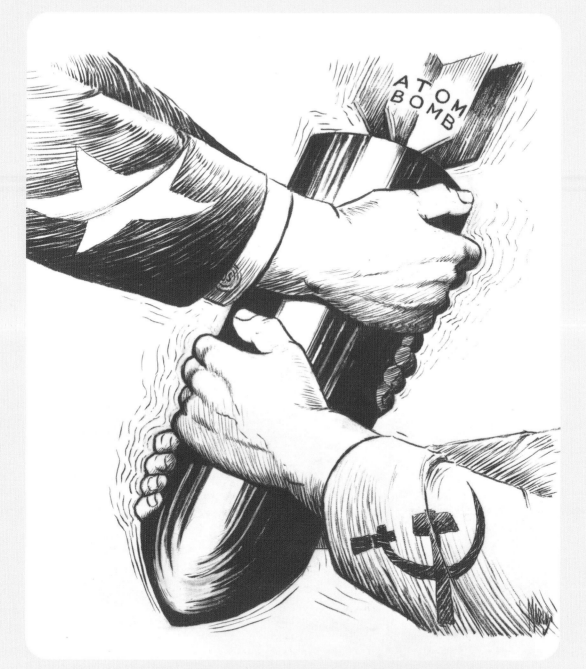

This 1949 cartoon neatly sums up the U.S.-Soviet struggle to get ahead in the arms race. Notice the "U.S." in the cufflink on the arm on the left. The hammer and sickle on the sleeve at right is the symbol of the Soviet Union.

American leaders. The Soviet bloc now included Poland, Czechoslovakia, Hungary, Romania, Bulgaria, and Albania. It seemed that without U.S. intervention, all of Europe could fall into Communist hands. Truman gave a speech to Congress, asking for immediate approval of the plan: "The Soviet Union and its agents have destroyed the independence and democratic character of a whole series of nations in Eastern and Central Europe. It is this ruthless course of action, and the clear design to extend it to the remaining free nations of Europe, that have brought about the critical situation in Europe today. The tragic death of the Republic of Czechoslovakia has sent a shock throughout the civilized world. Until the free nations of Europe have regained their strength, and so long as communism threatens the very existence of democracy, the United States must remain strong enough to support those countries of Europe which are threatened with communist control and police-state rule." Congress agreed and approved the Marshall Plan on April 3, 1948. The plan initially would send more than $5 billion in aid to Europe.

By the following June, the first major military crisis of the Cold War was under way, as leaders at the Kremlin—the Soviet seat of command in Moscow—cut off all supplies to West Berlin. By so doing, they hoped to force out Western troops. This act of aggression, together with the takeover in Czechoslovakia, helped crystallize plans to establish the North Atlantic Treaty Organization (NATO), a military alliance aimed at protecting Western nations from Soviet attack. NATO would be founded in April 1949. That same year, Communist revolutionaries took over the government of China. Another nation   one that had long been on friendly terms with the United States—was now Communist. Americans feared that communism was gaining ground.

To make matters worse, soon the United States would not be the only nation that possessed the atomic bomb. On August 29, 1949, the Soviet Union successfully detonated its first atomic bomb—several years sooner than U.S. experts had predicted it would. No longer could the United States consider its own technology a sufficient deterrent against war. Only four years after the end of World War II, the world was once again moving toward conflict. This time, people feared, it could truly be the war to end all wars. Anxiety over "the bomb" was building.

Leveling the Playing Field: The Soviets Successfully Test the A-Bomb

On September 21, 1949, President Truman's secretary of defense received a report informing him that the Soviets had detonated the A-bomb. Two days later, Truman announced the fact to the American people: "We have evidence that within recent weeks an atomic explosion occurred in the U.S.S.R." The following is the report to the secretary of defense.

MEMORANDUM BY THE CHIEF OF STAFF, U.S. AIR FORCE
TO THE SECRETARY OF DEFENSE ON LONG-RANGE DETECTION
OF ATOMIC EXPLOSIONS, 21 SEPTEMBER 1949

1. I believe that an atomic bomb has been detonated over the Asiatic land mass during the period 26 August 1949 to 29 August 1949. I

base this on positive information that has been obtained from the system established by the U.S. Air Force for the long range detection of foreign atomic energy activities.

2. Fission products have been collected since 3 September 1949. Although the system is only partially developed, we have been fortunate in securing sufficiently large and fresh samples for effective scientific analysis. The cloud containing fission products was tracked by the U.S. Air Force from the Kamchatka peninsula to the vicinity of the British Isles where it was also picked up by the Royal Air Force.

"I believe that an atomic bomb has been detonated over the Asiatic land mass."

3. Conclusions by our scientists based on physical and radiochemical analyses of collected data have been confirmed by scientists of the AEC, United Kingdom Office of Naval Research.

4. At my request, Dr. Vannevar Bush, Dr. J. Robert Oppenheimer, Dr. Robert Backer and Admiral William S. Parsons have reviewed our findings and concur unanimously in our conclusions.

5. The Joint Chiefs of Staff have been informed of the contents of this letter and the attached report.

—Memorandum by the Chief of Staff, U. S. Air Force to the Secretary of Defense on Long-Range Detection of Atomic Explosions, 21 September 1949.

THINK ABOUT THIS

1. How do you think U.S. officials and the American public reacted to this news?

2. The air force chief of staff noted that fission products, or radioactive fallout, were collected near the British Isles. Do you think that the testing of atomic weapons was acceptable, given that fallout could affect lands far from the actual explosion?

After the Soviets detonated their first bomb, the United States decided it needed to stay one step ahead of the enemy, regardless of the cost. In early 1951 Truman announced that U.S. scientists would continue to develop "all forms of atomic weapons, including the so-called hydrogen or superbomb" — a device approximately one thousand times more powerful than the A-bomb. Certainly U.S. leaders hoped never to use such a weapon. But what would happen if the Soviets had the capability and the United States did not?

On November 1, 1952, the U.S. detonated the first hydrogen bomb at Eniwetok Atoll in the Marshall Islands. Less than a year later, the USSR detonated its first H-bomb. The arms race was gaining momentum. In January 1954 President Dwight Eisenhower's secretary of state, John Foster Dulles, announced a new defense strategy, which came to be known as "massive retaliation." It marked a shift in emphasis: instead of relying mainly on traditional military forces to respond to an attack, the country would build up its supply of nuclear weapons.

November 1, 1952: The United States detonates the first hydrogen bomb, at Eniwetok Atoll in the Pacific. The radioactive smoke covered one hundred miles of sky with an ominous mushroom-shaped cloud.

The threat of retaliation with such powerful bombs would, it was hoped, deter any potential attackers. The following comes from Dulles's speech explaining the policy.

THE SOVIET COMMUNISTS . . . seek, through many types of maneuvers, gradually to divide and weaken the free nations by overextending them in efforts which, as Lenin put it, are "beyond their strength, so that they come to practical bankruptcy." Then, said Lenin, "our victory is assured." Then, said Stalin, will be "the moment for the decisive blow."

. . . it is not sound to become permanently committed to military expenditures so vast that they lead to "practical bankruptcy." . . .

We need allies and collective security. Our purpose is to make these relations more effective, less costly. This can be done by placing more reliance on deterrent power and less dependence on local defensive power.

"We want . . . a maximum deterrent at a bearable cost."

This is accepted practice so far as local communities are concerned. We keep locks on our doors, but we do not have an armed guard in every home. We rely principally on a community security system so well equipped to punish any who break in and steal that, in fact, would-be aggressors are generally deterred. That is the modern way of getting maximum protection at a bearable cost.

What the Eisenhower administration seeks is a similar international security system. We want, for ourselves and the other free nations, a maximum deterrent at a bearable cost.

Local defense will always be important. But there is no local defense which alone will contain the mighty landpower [military forces] of the Communist world. Local defenses must be reinforced by the further deterrent of massive retaliatory power. A potential aggressor must know that he cannot always prescribe battle conditions that suit him. Otherwise, for example, a potential aggressor, who is glutted with manpower, might be tempted to attack in confidence that resistance would be confined to manpower. He might be tempted to attack in places where his superiority was decisive.

The way to deter aggression is for the free community to be willing and able to respond vigorously at places and with means of its own choosing.

—From John Foster Dulles, "The Evolution of Foreign Policy,"
Department of State Bulletin *30 (January 25, 1962), pp. 107–110.*

THINK ABOUT THIS

1. What did Dulles mean by the terms *overextending* and *local defense*?
2. How would the policy of "massive retaliation" keep the Soviets from invading Western Europe?
3. What metaphor did Dulles use to explain the concept of deterrence?

Let the Space Race Begin!: *Sputnik* versus *Flopnik*

In the early years of the arms race, the United States led the way, and the Soviets followed. But on October 4, 1957, the first satellite, named *Sputnik* (which means "fellow traveler"), was launched into space from a Soviet base. Americans were shocked—and frightened. Citizens, scientists, and leaders alike had assumed that the United States would be the first to reach outer space. How might the Soviets put this new technology to use? Americans knew that if the Soviets could launch a satellite into space, they were capable of developing nuclear missiles that could reach the United States as well. The nation was on edge, and

4 ОКТЯБРЯ
в Советском Союзе произведен
запуск ПЕРВОГО искусственного
СПУТНИКА ЗЕМЛИ

3 НОЯБРЯ
в Советском Союзе произведен
запуск ВТОРОГО искусственного
СПУТНИКА ЗЕМЛИ

A Soviet illustration celebrates the launches of *Sputnik I* and *Sputnik II* in 1957.

the pressure was on to speed up the U.S. space program.

Indeed, two months after *Sputnik,* on December 6, the United States did attempt to launch its first satellite—with disastrous results. Here, a front-page article from the London *Daily Herald* recounts the event.

OH, WHAT A FLOPNIK!
Satellite Blows Up before Take-off
by Gilbert Carter

America's much-ballyhooed bid to launch a satellite to join Russia's two Sputniks in space ended yesterday in a huge billow of orange flame—on the ground.

For the tiny, 6lb. missile—which will go down in history as the

Flopnik—died bleeding a message of failure as its three stage rocket blew up on the launching ramp.

It happened at Cape Canaveral, Florida, where America's scientific reputation lay at stake because of the world-wide publicity given to this attempt to keep up with the Joneskis.

—From Gilbert Carter, *"Oh, What a Flopnik!"* Daily Herald, *December 7, 1957, p. 1.*

THINK ABOUT THIS

1. How do you think Americans responded to the failure of the U.S. satellite?

2. What did the author mean by the phrase "keep up with the Joneskis"?

It's MADness: The Secretary of Defense Explains Mutual Assured Destruction

Deterrence continued to be the key strategy throughout the Cold War. Whenever the two powers stumbled toward conflict—and they did on several occasions—the possibility of worldwide destruction loomed. The United States and the Soviet Union tried to establish some control over the arms race. In the Nuclear Test Ban Treaty of 1963, for example, Great Britain, the United States, and the Soviet Union agreed to halt all but underground testing of nuclear weapons. Five years later the three nations signed another agreement, the Nuclear Non-Proliferation Treaty of July 1968, which prohibited transfer of nuclear technology to other nations. These were but small steps in the process of disarmament, yet they opened discussion on arms limitation—a topic that is still of importance today. At the end of the 1960s, however, it was not treaties but the so-called MAD, or mutual assured destruction, doctrine that kept the world free from nuclear war. According to MAD, both superpowers knew that an attack would guarantee retaliation of equal or greater force. Knowing few people would survive a nuclear war meant that leaders on both sides had to do everything in their power to prevent it. But mutual deterrence also meant that the arms race would continue—with or without treaties. In the passage that follows, Robert McNamara, the secretary of defense under Presidents Kennedy and Johnson, outlines the concept of mutual assured destruction.

IN A COMPLEX AND UNCERTAIN WORLD, the gravest problem that an American Secretary of Defense must face is that of planning, preparation and policy against the possibility of thermonuclear war. It is a prospect that most of mankind understandably would prefer not to contemplate. For technology has now circumscribed us all with a horizon of horror that could dwarf any catastrophe that has befallen man in his more than a million years on earth.

Man has lived now for more than twenty years in what we have come to call the Atomic Age. What we sometimes overlook is that every future age of man will be an atomic age, and if man is to have a future at all, it will have to be one overshadowed with the permanent possibility of thermonuclear holocaust. About that fact there is no longer any doubt. Our freedom in this question consists only in facing the matter rationally and realistically and discussing actions to minimize the danger.

No sane citizen, political leader or nation wants thermonuclear war. But merely not wanting it is not enough. We must understand the differences among actions which increase its risks, those which reduce them and those which, while costly, have little influence one way or another. But there is a great difficulty in the way of constructive and profitable debate over the issues, and that is the exceptional complexity of nuclear strategy. Unless these complexities are well understood rational discussion and decision-making are impossible.

One must begin with precise definitions. The cornerstone of our strategic policy continues to be to deter nuclear attack upon the United States or its allies. We do this by maintaining a

". . . a highly reliable ability to inflict unacceptable damage"

highly reliable ability to inflict unacceptable damage upon any single aggressor or combination of aggressors at any time during the course of a strategic nuclear exchange, even after absorbing a surprise first strike. This can be defined as our assured-destruction capability.

It is important to understand that assured destruction is the very essence of the whole deterrence concept. We must possess an actual assured-destruction capability, and that capability also must be credible. The point is that a potential aggressor must believe that our assured-destruction capability is in fact actual, and that our will to use it in retaliation to an attack is in fact unwavering. The conclusion, then, is clear: if the United States is to deter a nuclear attack on itself or its allies, it must possess an actual and a credible assured-destruction capability.

—*From Secretary of Defense Robert S. McNamara, speech given September 18, 1967.*

THINK ABOUT THIS

According to McNamara, what factors were necessary for the MAD strategy to work?

In June of 1948, the Russians began an eleven-month blockade of roads and waterways leading into Berlin from West Germany. Here children in West Berlin look on as fleets of U.S. airplanes transport supplies to the city, circumventing the blockade.

Chapter 3

Cold War Battlegrounds: Conflict across the Globe

ALTHOUGH THE AMERICANS AND SOVIETS never actually faced each other in battle during the Cold War, they clashed indirectly throughout the era. Around the world, from Asia to Africa, Europe to South America, battlegrounds erupted wherever Communists sought to spread their beliefs and Westerners—in particular, the United States—vowed to stop them.

The first of these conflicts arose in Germany, shortly after the end of World War II. Ever since the nation and its capital had been divided, there was competition between East and West for control. In 1948 the United States, Great Britain, and France—the Western powers—agreed to a plan that would eventually combine their three occupation zones into one. The new political entity, West Germany, would have its own government and would receive aid under the Marshall Plan. In addition, the new state would have its own currency, the deutsche mark. The Soviets were outraged. To them, these actions were a clear attempt on the part of the West to control Germany. It took little time for them to retaliate.

Berlin lay deep inside the Soviet zone, but, like the country as a whole, the capital city had been divided into four sectors overseen by the four Allied powers. At the Potsdam Conference, officials had determined specific land and air routes for free travel into and out of Berlin. In June 1948, in an effort to oust Western troops from the city, the Soviets imposed a blockade. Barriers closed road, rail, and canal traffic linking Berlin with West Germany. Electricity was also cut off. Food and other supplies had always come to the Western sectors from the Western powers, so the people of West Berlin were in grave danger. The Soviets' intention was clear: either the Western powers would change their policies, or they would be forced out of Berlin.

What could be done? Officials in the British Royal Air Force came up with the idea of supplying the city by air. Americans agreed to work with the British on the project, and the first U.S. transport plane flew over Berlin on June 26, 1948. The Soviets did little to stop the airlift, at first because they doubted such an effort could ever succeed. Later they allowed it to continue, fearing that any interference would lead to war. At that time the United States was still the only country to have harnessed the power of atomic energy, and this was a powerful incentive to avoid war.

The airlift would continue for nearly a year, until the blockade was lifted on May 12, 1949, largely because the West's counter-blockade had kept steel and coal shipments from entering East Berlin, hurting Soviet attempts to build industry in their sector. By the end of the year, Germany was officially two countries: the democratic Federal Republic of Germany (or West Germany) and the communist German Democratic Republic (or East Germany).

Americans viewed the end of the blockade as a victory, and

many thought it was the end of the Cold War. It was not. By the end of August, the Soviets had tested their first atomic bomb. In 1950, when war broke out in Korea between communist and capitalist forces, it seemed there was no end in sight to conflict.

Blockade! An Airlift Saves West Berlin

Following is a front-page article from a *New York Times* correspondent in Berlin, who reported the plan to deliver supplies to the people of Berlin by air, an effort that soon became known as Operation Vittles.

BERLIN, JUNE 26—United States airpower throughout Europe is being mobilized for a great shuttle service into besieged Berlin. United States aircraft, which four years ago brought death to the city, will bring life in the form of food and medicines to the people of the Western sectors, whose food supplies have been cut off by the Russians. . . .

The air food shipments are not intended to meet any immediate need but to augment the existing stocks and to insure that the Germans receive a balanced diet, United States Military Government sources said. . . .

The official view is that under the present conditions the people of the three Western sectors of the city, whose regular supply has been cut by the Soviet Military Administration, can be fed for thirty days on the existing stocks plus the goods flown in by air.

"The situation will become really serious around the end of July," according to a senior official. . . .

But although the United States and Britain are making every preparation to withstand a siege of that length, many senior officials believe the Russian restrictions will be lifted before then. . . .

This contrasts sharply with the official view of the German Communists expressed this morning by Wilhelm Pleck, co-chairman of the Soviet-sponsored Socialist Unity party. Herr Pleck said at a press conference that the Berlin crisis would be settled only when the Western Allies left Berlin. . . .

"...the Soviet Military Administration is systematically starving 2,500,000 persons in Berlin."

But some observers say it is difficult to see how the Russian propagandists, no matter how adroit, will be able to explain away the fact that the Soviet Military Administration is systematically starving 2,500,000 persons in Berlin. Such slogans as "the solidarity of the working classes" are said to be in sharp variance with the brutality of the Russian measures.

One interesting point made today by a senior United States Military Government official was that although the Russians had barred the shipment of food by rail, highway and waterway into Berlin, these routes were not closed permanently by Russian order but in each case "temporarily" for "technical reasons."

Thus the Soviet Military Administration has left itself an out if the pressure of world opinion and Western economic sanctions become too great.

—From Drew Middleton, *"U.S. Will Mobilize Planes in Europe to Supply Berlin,"*
New York Times, *June 27, 1948, p. 1.*

THINK ABOUT THIS

1. What was ironic about Americans helping the people of Berlin during the blockade?

2. What statements did the reporter make that showed his negative feelings about communism and the Soviet Union?

3. According to the reporter, how did the Soviets leave themselves an "out" if the world was critical of the blockade?

A Pilot Thinks of the Children

Within no time, hundreds of U.S. pilots were sent to Germany to command planes carrying food, medicine, and coal to Berlin. On September 18 a record 7,000 tons of supplies were delivered in a single day, and by that time a total of 200,000 tons had made it to the citizens of Berlin. One pilot, Gail S. Halvorsen, thought the children of Berlin could use something more. Using tiny parachutes made from handkerchiefs, he and his crew began dropping "bombs" of chocolate and gum from their plane down to the city below. As news of "Operation Little Vittles" reached the United States, huge quantities of sweets and handkerchiefs were sent to help the cause. Soon other countries chipped in, too. Following is an excerpt from Halvorsen's book, recounting the event that led to his efforts. While walking in Berlin one day, Halvorsen stopped to chat with a few German children, but as he turned to leave, he had a thought.

INSTINCTIVELY I REACHED IN MY POCKET. There had been no preparation for such a moment. All there were was two sticks of Wrigley's Doublemint gum.

Thirty kids and two sticks, there will be a fight. . . .

I broke the two sticks of gum in half and headed for the children. . . .

The four pieces were quickly placed. In all my experience, including Christmases past, I had never witnessed such an expression of surprise, joy, and sheer pleasure that I beheld in the eyes and faces of those four young people. Nor do I remember seeing such disappointment as was evident in the eyes of those who came so close. The

Excited children—and even a few adults—reach for candy dropped as part of "Operation Little Vittles."

disappointed looks were transitory and tempered by their much more difficult trials and disappointments over the past month. The pleased looks of the four were frozen in time. . . .

I must have been a sight, standing there in wide mouthed amazement. What I could do with 30 full sticks of gum! . . .

Just then another C-54 [jet] swooped over our heads, across the fence and landed. . . . That plane gave me a sudden flash of inspiration.

Why not drop some gum and even chocolate to these kids out of our airplane the next daylight trip to Berlin?

—From Gail S. Halvorsen, The Berlin Candy Bomber, *pp. 102–104.*
Bountiful, UT: Horizon Publishers, 2002.

A Presidential Candidate Vows to End the Korean War

At the close of World War II, the Soviet Union and United States took control of Korea, which had been occupied by Japan for decades. Korea was divided in half along the thirty-eighth parallel; Soviets occupied the north, Americans the south. On June 25, 1950, with strategic help and munitions from the Soviets, Communist North Korea invaded South Korea, planning to reunite the nation as a single communist state. Although the Soviets denied involvement, officials in Washington were certain they were behind the invasion. Of the threat in Korea, President Truman said, "The Communists in the Kremlin are engaged in a monstrous conspiracy to stamp out freedom all over the world." He sent U.S. troops to stop the invasion, and for the first time Americans faced communist forces—not Soviet but Korean and later Chinese. The war was more difficult than expected, particularly once the Chinese entered the conflict. And coming so soon on the heels of the worst war in history, it was no wonder that Americans wanted out of Korea. As Dwight Eisenhower campaigned for the presidency in the fall of 1952, he promised an end to the conflict in Korea. Following are portions of a famous campaign speech that he delivered to the people of Detroit, Michigan.

IN THIS ANXIOUS AUTUMN FOR AMERICA, one fact looms above all others in our people's mind. One tragedy challenges all men dedicated to the work of peace. One word shouts denial to those who foolishly pretend that ours is not a nation at war.

This fact, this tragedy, this word is: Korea.

A small country—Korea has been, for more than two years, the battleground for the costliest foreign war our nation has fought, excepting the two World Wars. It has been the burial ground for 20,000 American dead. It has been another historic field of honor for the valor and skill and tenacity of American soldiers.

All these things it has been—and yet one thing more. It has been a symbol—a telling symbol—of the foreign policy of our nation.

It has been a sign—a warning sign—of the way the administration has conducted our world affairs.

It has been a measure— a damning measure—of the quality of leadership we have been given. . . .

The first task of a new administration will be to review and re-examine every course of action open to us with one goal in view: to bring the Korean War to an early and honorable end. That is my pledge to the American people.

Dwight D. Eisenhower was a popular general and hero of World War II, and his 1952 presidential campaign would be a tremendous success. He is shown here after winning the election.

For this task a wholly new administration is necessary. The reason for this is simple. The old administration cannot be expected to repair what it failed to prevent.

Where will the new administration begin? . . .

I shall go to Korea.

That is my second pledge to the American people.

—From "Address by Dwight D. Eisenhower, Republican Nominee for President, Delivered at Detroit, Michigan, October 24, 1952." The Dwight D. Eisenhower Library, National Archives and Records Administration. To read the speech in its entirety, visit http://www.eisenhower.utexas.edu/Korea/html/Koreandocuments.html

THINK ABOUT THIS

1. Congress had never formally declared war in Korea; the action was called only a "conflict." Why therefore might Eisenhower's opening words have been powerful?

2. Eisenhower was a great general during World War II. Why might his position, that of ending the Korean conflict, been popular with Americans?

Crisis in Cuba: The CIA's Top-Secret Plan

The Korean War came to an end with the signing of a settlement on July 27, 1953. Communism in Korea would never move south of the thirty-eighth parallel, but the threat in Asia was not over. Ten months after the peace talks ended in Korea, Vietnam—formerly a French colony—won its independence. Communist guerrillas had long been fighting for control of the Southeast Asian nation. With the French withdrawal, the country was divided into two parts— the Communists in the north and the capitalist forces in the south. Americans watched events unfold with growing apprehension.

At the same time, a Communist rebel named Fidel Castro was

American leaders considered Castro—shown here in 1960 speaking to reporters—a tremendous threat. A Communist regime a mere ninety miles from American shores was an unacceptable challenge to U.S. interests.

rallying troops on the island of Cuba, just off the coast of Florida. In 1959, after a six-year guerrilla war, he took control of the island nation. By the following year, his government was an ally of the Soviet Union and Communist China. Shipments of Soviet weapons began to reach the shores of Cuba.

Cuba was much too close for American comfort. Eisenhower secretly approved a Central Intelligence Agency (CIA) program to train a paramilitary force of Cuban exiles. The plan was that they would invade Cuba and form a resistance movement that would gain the support of the Cuban people. Eventually they would be powerful enough to topple Castro and his regime. Following is a portion of a top-secret CIA document detailing the plan.

OBJECTIVE: The purpose of the program outlined herein is to bring about the replacement of the Castro regime with one more devoted to the true interests of the Cuban people and more acceptable to the U.S. in such a manner as to avoid any appearance of U.S. intervention. Essentially the method of accomplishing this end will be to induce, support, and so far as possible direct action, both inside and outside of Cuba, by selected groups of Cubans of a sort that they might be expected to and could undertake on their own initiative.

"The purpose . . . is to bring about the replacement of the Castro regime."

Since a crisis inevitably entailing drastic action in or toward Cuba could be provoked by circumstances beyond control of the U.S. before the covert action program has accomplished its objective, every effort will be made to carry it out in such a way as progressively to improve the capability of the U.S. to act in a crisis.

—From "A Program of Covert Action against the Castro Regime," Central Intelligence Agency, March 16, 1960. To read the document in its entirety, visit http://www.parascope.com/articles/1296/baydocs.htm

THINK ABOUT THIS

1. Do you think U.S. officials were more concerned with the interests of the Cuban people or with removing a communist government from a neighboring country?

2. Why did the United States decide to use Cuban paramilitary forces in this operation?

3. Do you believe that one nation has the right to overthrow the government of another nation?

Chapter 4

Turbulent Times:
War Rages into the Sixties

EISENHOWER WOULD NOT BE IN THE OVAL OFFICE to see the results of his decision to train Cuban resistance fighters, for his two terms as president were ending. In 1961 the new president, John F. Kennedy, inherited the Cold War—including a crisis in Cuba, a new threat brewing in Berlin, and a troubling situation in Vietnam.

Although Kennedy began his term with positive ideas for change, he faced many challenges, as did his successor, Lyndon B. Johnson. The 1960s saw few signs of improved relations between the United States and the Soviet Union. Nonetheless, on the day Kennedy was sworn into office the country felt, for a brief moment, that perhaps the Cold War would begin to thaw.

The day before Kennedy was inaugurated, in January 1961, Eisenhower briefed him on a number of topics. It was then that he learned of the plan to invade Cuba. Three months later, approximately 1,400 men—all Cuban exiles—attempted to invade the Caribbean island at the Bay of Pigs. The rebel forces were relatively small in number, however, and lacked the training to carry out the

Cause for alarm: Cuba's Fidel Castro and Soviet leader
Nikita Khrushchev embrace.

attack successfully. Cuban government troops quickly crushed the invasion. The events helped to unify the Cuban people behind Castro's leadership, and, for the first time, he officially proclaimed Cuba a communist nation. Its ally, the Soviet Union, immediately promised support should the United States attack.

During the year and a half that followed the Bay of Pigs invasion, tensions between the superpowers escalated, finally culminating in the Cuban Missile Crisis. Lasting thirteen terrifying days, the Cuban Missile Crisis brought the United States and the Soviet Union the closest they would ever come to nuclear annihilation.

The crisis began in October 1962 when U.S. officials learned that the Soviet Union had secretly set up missile bases in Cuba, a step that offered advantages far beyond simply protecting the small island nation from U.S. aggression.

Before their alliance with Cuba, the Soviets had no missiles located outside their borders, nor did they have the technology to send a missile across the Atlantic to North America. They were, however, acutely aware that the United States had nuclear weapons based in Turkey that could wipe out three of their major cities—Kiev, Minsk, and Moscow—in a matter of minutes. Soviet leader Nikita Khrushchev, who had come to power in 1958, realized that placing Soviet missiles in Cuba would have two advantages: Cuba would be protected from invasion, and the balance of power with the United States would be equalized.

On Sunday morning, October 14, 1962, an American U-2 spy plane photographed the missile sites, which were still under construction. That night Kennedy's national security adviser was informed of the unthinkable: Soviet missiles were about to be set up ninety miles from U.S. soil. Kennedy and his advisers soon learned that the Soviets planned to install missiles that could reach every major American city except Seattle, which lay far away from Cuba in the Pacific Northwest. The United States was in grave danger.

Kennedy and his aides considered an air strike on the Soviet bases in Cuba, but this could lead to a deadly conflict. After days of deliberation, Kennedy decided to enact a blockade of Cuba, which he called a quarantine. One hundred and eighty U.S. Navy warships would circle around the island, ensuring that the Soviets could send no additional armaments or manpower. In preparation for war, U.S. aircraft were armed with nuclear weapons; U.S. nuclear submarines were stationed at sea. The Cuban Missile Crisis was only the beginning of a turbulent decade that would lead Americans to question the ongoing commitment to the nuclear arsenal—and to fighting communism.

"This Much We Pledge": Kennedy Promises a Fresh Start

Following is a selection from President Kennedy's inaugural address. His words acknowledged that the Cold War was far from over. But he believed both sides had a responsibility to move beyond the past to forge a better world.

LET EVERY NATION KNOW, whether it wishes us well or ill, that we shall pay any price, bear any burden, meet any hardship, support any friend, oppose any foe to assure the survival and the success of liberty.

MEDIUM RANGE BALLISTIC MISSILE BASE IN CUBA

SAN CRISTOBAL

LAUNCH POSITION

MISSILE-READY TENTS

MISSILE ERECTORS

As Kennedy entered office, he could not have predicted that by October of the following year U.S.–Soviet relations would have reached an all-time low. These aerial spy photos clearly show a Soviet missile base in San Cristóbal, Cuba.

This much we pledge—and more.

To those old allies whose cultural and spiritual origins we share, we pledge the loyalty of faithful friends. . . .

To those new states whom we welcome to the ranks of the free, we pledge our word that one form of colonial control shall not have passed away merely to be replaced by a far more iron tyranny. We shall not always expect to find them supporting our view. But we shall always hope to find them strongly supporting their own freedom—and to remember that, in the past, those who foolishly sought power by riding the back of the tiger ended up inside. . . .

To our sister republics south of our border, we offer a special pledge—to convert our good words into good deeds—in a new alliance for progress—to assist free men and free governments in casting off the chains of poverty. But this peaceful revolution of hope cannot become the prey of hostile powers. Let all our neighbors know that we shall join with them to oppose aggression or subversion any where in the Americas. And let every other power know that this Hemisphere intends to remain the master of its own house. . . .

Finally, to those nations who would make themselves our adversary, we offer not a pledge but a request: that both sides begin anew the quest for peace, before the dark powers of destruction unleashed by science engulf all humanity in planned or accidental self-destruction.

We dare not tempt them with weakness. For only when our arms are sufficient beyond doubt can we be certain beyond doubt that they will never be employed.

But neither can two great and powerful groups of nations take comfort from our present course—both sides overburdened by the cost of modern weapons, both rightly alarmed by the steady spread of the deadly atom, yet both racing to alter that uncertain balance of terror that stays the hand of mankind's final war.

So let us begin anew. . . .

Let both sides explore what problems unite us instead of belaboring those problems which divide us.

"Let both sides seek to invoke the wonders of science instead of its terrors."

Let both sides, for the first time, formulate serious and precise proposals for the inspection and control of arms—and bring the absolute power to destroy other nations under the absolute control of all nations.

Let both sides seek to invoke the wonders of science instead of its terrors. Together let us explore the stars, conquer the deserts, eradicate disease, tap the ocean depths and encourage the arts and commerce.

—From "Inaugural Address," President John F. Kennedy, Washington, D.C., January 20, 1961. To read and listen to Kennedy deliver the full speech, visit the Kennedy Library: http://www.cs.umb.edu/jfklibrary/j012061.htm

1. Kennedy spoke to people all over the world in his inaugural address. Can you give examples of specific countries he might have had in mind? For example, did he say anything that might have been directed toward Cuba? Or toward Vietnam, a former French colony?

2. Did Kennedy believe the United States should stop producing nuclear weapons? How did he suggest the country might best deal with the arms race?

Khrushchev and Kennedy Exchange Words: The Bay of Pigs

Following the Bay of Pigs invasion, a displeased Chairman Khrushchev exchanged communications with President Kennedy about the situation in Cuba. Portions of their telegrams follow.

TELEGRAM FROM CHAIRMAN KHRUSHCHEV TO PRESIDENT KENNEDY, APRIL 18, 1961—

I approach you, Mr. President, with an urgent call to put an end to aggression against the Republic of Cuba. Military armament and the world political situation are such at this time that any so-called "little war" can touch off a chain reaction in all parts of the globe.

As far as the Soviet Union is concerned, there should be no mistake about our position: We will render the Cuban people and their government all necessary help to repel armed attack on Cuba. We are sincerely interested in a relaxation of international tension, but if others proceed toward sharpening, we will answer them in full measure. . . .

I hope that the Government of the USA will consider our views as dictated by the sole concern not to allow steps which could lead the world to military catastrophe.

Following the rise of the Castro regime, many Cubans sought refuge in the United States. In this photograph from April 17, 1961, anxious members of Miami's large Cuban population listen to the radio for reports on the progress of the Bay of Pigs invasion.

TELEGRAM FROM PRESIDENT KENNEDY TO CHAIRMAN KHRUSHCHEV, APRIL 18, 1961—

Mr. Chairman: You are under a serious misapprehension in regard to events in Cuba. For months there has been evident and growing resistance to the Castro dictatorship. . . .

I have previously stated, and I repeat now, that the United States intends no military intervention in Cuba. . . . While refraining from military intervention in Cuba, the people of the United States do not conceal their admiration for Cuban patriots who wish to see a democratic system in an independent Cuba. The United States Government can take no action to stifle the spirit of liberty.

I have taken careful note of your statement that the events in Cuba might affect peace in all parts of the world. I trust that this does not mean that the Soviet Government, using the situation in Cuba as a pretext, is planning to inflame other areas of the world. I would like to think that your government has too great a sense of responsibility to embark upon any enterprise so dangerous to general peace. . . .

"The great revolution in the history of man . . . is the revolution of those determined to be free."

I believe, Mr. Chairman, that you should recognize that free peoples in all parts of the world do not accept the claim of historical inevitability for Communist revolution. What your government believes is its own business; what it does in the world is the world's business. The great revolution in the history of man, past, present and future, is the revolution of those determined to be free.

—*From* Foreign Relations of the United States, 1961–1963, *Volume X, Cuba, 1961–1962; Washington, DC: U.S. Department of State.*

Think about This

1. Did Kennedy admit to U.S. involvement in the Bay of Pigs affair?
2. How did Khrushchev threaten to retaliate if the United States took action in Cuba?
3. What did Kennedy mean by the "historical inevitability for Communist revolution"?

Kennedy in Troubled Berlin

In 1961 the city of Berlin was once again a pressure point of Cold War hostility. Communist leaders wanted the West out of Berlin. They also wanted to stem the growing tide of refugees from East Berlin who crossed the border into the Western sector, escaping to freedom. East Berlin was losing citizens—workers and trained professionals who were needed to ensure the city's survival. Leaders at the Kremlin decided there was only one remedy: close all access in East Berlin to the West. In the dark of night on August 13, the clamor of trucks and machinery awoke the people of Berlin. As the sun rose the following morning, one could see what was happening: troops were erecting concrete posts and barbed wire to barricade East Berlin. Just beyond the city, Soviet tanks stood at the ready lest anyone protest. By the end of the day, 103 miles of barbed wire separated East and West Berlin, dividing families and friends, tearing the city in two. Soon the government erected a more permanent wall of brick and concrete. East Berlin was a prison, the Berlin Wall the ultimate symbol of the division between East and West. In June 1963 Kennedy visited West Berlin at the end of a trip to West Germany. He spoke to a crowd of one million Berliners, overlooking a square that would later bear his name.

THERE ARE MANY PEOPLE IN THE WORLD who really don't understand, or say they don't, what is the great issue between the free world and the Communist world. Let them come to Berlin. There are some who say that communism is the wave of the future. Let them come to Berlin. And there are some who say in Europe and elsewhere we can

There would be many attempts to scale the Berlin Wall in search of freedom on the other side. ABOVE: A border guard steals an opportunity to escape. RIGHT: Many such attempts ended in tragedy. Here a young man, just steps away from freedom, was shot and killed as he tried to make it over the wall.

work with the Communists. Let them come to Berlin. And there are even a few who say that it is true that communism is an evil system, but it permits us to make economic progress. *Lass' sie nach Berlin kommen.* Let them come to Berlin.

Freedom has many difficulties and democracy is not perfect, but we have never had to put a wall up to keep our people in, to prevent them from leaving us. . . . While the wall is the most obvious and vivid demonstration of the failures of the Communist system, for all the world to see, we take no satisfaction in it, for it is, as your Mayor has said, an offense not only against history but an offense against humanity, separating families, dividing husbands and wives and brothers and sisters, and dividing a people who wish to be joined together. . . .

Freedom is indivisible, and when one man is enslaved, all are not free. When all are free, then we can look forward to that day when this city will be joined as one and this country and this great Continent of Europe in a peaceful and hopeful globe. When that day finally comes, as it will, the people of West Berlin can take sober satisfaction in the fact that they were in the front lines for almost two decades.

"Ich bin ein Berliner."

All free men, wherever they may live, are citizens of Berlin, and, therefore, as a free man, I take pride in the words "Ich bin ein Berliner" [I am a Berliner].

—From President John F. Kennedy, remarks in the Rudolph Wilde Platz, West Berlin, June 26, 1963.

THINK ABOUT THIS

1. How could the Berlin Wall be viewed as a demonstration that communism did not work?

2. Why do you think Kennedy chose to use German phrases in his speech? What did he mean by the sentence *Ich bin ein Berliner*—"I am a Berliner"?

On the Edge: Attorney General Robert F. Kennedy Recalls the Cuban Missile Crisis

Throughout the arms race, as Americans and Soviets stockpiled weapons, it often seemed as if nuclear war was inevitable. In the fall of 1962 the nation was at the brink. On Wednesday, October 24, Russian ships neared the naval barrier that Kennedy had imposed around Cuba. The president had to decide whether, if the Soviets tried to break through, U.S. ships would fire or withdraw. To withdraw would mean defeat; to stop them would be the first step to nuclear war. The president's brother and closest adviser, Attorney General Robert F. Kennedy, was among the aides who helped Kennedy make the difficult decisions of those anxious days. His memoir, *Thirteen Days,* tells of the events during that time. In the following passage he describes the most dangerous moments of the crisis.

THIS WAS THE MOMENT WE HAD PREPARED FOR, which we hoped would never come. The danger and concern that we all felt hung like a cloud over us all and particularly over the President. . . .

It was now a few minutes after 10:00 o'clock. Secretary McNamara announced that two Russian ships, the *Gagarin* and the *Komiles,* were within a few miles of our quarantine barrier. . . .

Then came the disturbing Navy report that a Russian submarine had moved into position between the two ships. . . .

I think these few minutes were the time of gravest concern for the President. Was the world on the brink of a holocaust? Was it our error? A mistake? Was there something further that should have been done? Or not done? His hand went up to his face and covered his mouth. He opened and closed his fist. His face seemed drawn, his eyes pained, almost gray. We stared at each other across the table. For a few fleeting seconds, it was almost as though no one else was there and he was no longer the President. . . .

We had come to the time of final decision. "We must expect that they will close down Berlin—make the final preparations for that," the President said. I felt we were on the edge of a precipice with no way off. This time, the moment was now—not next week—not tomorrow, "so we can have another meeting and decide"; not in eight hours, "so we can send another message to Khrushchev and perhaps he will finally understand."

No, none of that was possible. One thousand miles away in the vast expanse of the Atlantic Ocean, the final decisions were going to be made in the next few minutes. President Kennedy had initiated the course of events, but he no longer had control over them. He would have to wait—we would have to wait. The minutes in the Cabinet Room slowly ticked by. What could we say now—what could we do?

Then it was 10:25—a messenger brought in a note to [director of Central Intelligence] John McCone. "Mr. President, we have a preliminary

President Kennedy *(right)* confers with his brother Robert at the White House in October 1962, during the buildup of tensions that preceded the Cuban Missile Crisis.

report which seems to indicate that some of the Russian ships stopped dead in the water."

The meeting droned on. But everyone looked like a different person. For a moment the world had stood still, and now it was going around again.

—From Robert F. Kennedy, Thirteen Days: A Memoir of the Cuban Missile Crisis. *New York: W. W. Norton & Company, 1969, pp. 68–72.*

THINK ABOUT THIS

1. How could an attack on the Russian ships have led to problems in Berlin?
2. What was the significance of the Russian ships having stopped in the water?

A War in Vietnam: The State Department Issues a Report

The Cuban Missile Crisis was not the only Cold War dilemma of the 1960s. According to the Truman Doctrine, the United States was committed to preventing the spread of communism across the globe, and Vietnam appeared to be the next stop. In 1965, as the United States stepped up military support for the South Vietnamese against the North Vietnamese Communists, the State Department issued a report, a portion of which follows here.

SOUTH VIETNAM IS FIGHTING FOR ITS LIFE against a brutal campaign of terror and armed attack inspired, directed, supplied, and controlled by the Communist regime in Hanoi. This flagrant aggression has been going on for years, but recently the pace has quickened and the threat has now become acute. . . .

In Vietnam a Communist government has set out deliberately to conquer a sovereign people in a neighboring state. And to achieve its end, it has used every resource of its own government to carry out its carefully planned program of concealed aggression. . . .

"South Vietnam is fighting for its life."

The directing force behind the effort to conquer South Vietnam is the Communist Party in the North, the Lao Dong (Workers) Party. As in every Communist state, the party is an integral part of the regime itself. North Vietnamese officials have expressed their firm determination to absorb South Vietnam into the Communist world. . . .

The United States seeks no territory, no military bases, no favored position. But we have learned the meaning of aggression elsewhere in the post-war world, and we have met it.

If peace can be restored in South Vietnam, the United States will be ready at once to reduce its military involvement. But it will not abandon friends who want to remain free. It will do what must be done to help them. The choice now between peace and continued and increasingly destructive conflict is one for the authorities in Hanoi to make.

—From *"Aggression from the North," State Department White Paper on Vietnam, February 27, 1965. Published in* Department of State Bulletin, *March 22, 1965.*

THINK ABOUT THIS

1. According to this report, why were American forces sent to Vietnam?

2. The report says the Communists in Vietnam were trying to conquer a neighboring state. How do you think the North Vietnamese would have described their actions?

Chapter 5

Thaw and Freeze

THE CUBAN MISSILE CRISIS ENDED with Kennedy promising not to invade Cuba and to end the blockade if Khrushchev removed all missiles from the island. Kennedy also promised to remove missiles from Turkey, but this was to remain a secret until America's NATO allies were consulted and brought in on the deal. To the world, it appeared that the United States had won the standoff, and Kennedy was a hero. But one thing was clear to both sides: the superpowers must never come so close to nuclear war again.

The arms race was draining coffers on both sides of the Cold War. Soviets and Americans needed to find a way to coexist. In August 1963 the United States and the Soviet Union, as well as Great Britain, signed the Test Ban Treaty, which limited the testing of nuclear weapons. In October 1964 the People's Republic of China successfully tested its first nuclear bomb. By this time the Soviets and Chinese were far from friendly, in part because the Soviets had refused to pass on technology for China to build a nuclear bomb. China persisted without their help. With a new

The late sixties and early seventies would see signs of improvement in superpower relations. Following the high-pressure anxiety of the Cuban Missile Crisis, Americans and Soviets seemed ready for an easing of tensions, and these sentiments gave rise to a policy known as détente. President Richard Nixon *(right)* and his Soviet counterpart Leonid Brezhnev are shown here conversing during a 1974 summit meeting.

player in the "nuclear club," one hostile to both superpowers, the world became that much more dangerous. The situation provided additional incentive for Soviets and Americans to come to terms.

Lyndon B. Johnson had become president in November 1963, after the tragic assassination of John F. Kennedy. Most of Johnson's time was occupied by the conflict in Vietnam, which would prove to be futile and exhausting for the nation. Many Americans, especially young people, opposed the war. Protest marches and demonstrations were held around the country. As the war dragged on, it seemed that fewer Americans—of any age—were willing to send the nation's young men across the globe to battle communism. The Vietnam War escalated into one of the most painful in U.S. history, galvanizing American public opinion toward peace—in Vietnam and on the symbolic battleground of the Cold War. Sadly, it would be many years before the Vietnam conflict would end, in April 1975.

The trend toward easing tensions between the superpowers eventually led to a policy known as détente, which was marked by efforts on both sides to improve relations. Détente took hold in 1969, as President Richard Nixon entered office. There were bumps in the road, as when the Soviets and the United States took opposite sides in a conflict in the Middle East between Egypt and Israel. But there were important steps toward peace as well. Nixon and Soviet leader Leonid Brezhnev signed the Strategic Arms Limitation Talks (SALT) treaty in 1972. They also agreed to the Anti-Ballistic Missile (ABM) Treaty, which restricted the use of antiballistic missiles. ABMs can shoot down incoming missiles before they strike. Both sides believed such technology was a dangerous threat to deterrence because it could remove the threat of "massive retaliation." For example, if the United States had possessed an ABM, the technology could have destroyed a Soviet weapon before it could do any damage. U.S. leaders would have known their nation was invulnerable to a Soviet assault, allowing them to launch a surprise attack without fear of retaliation. Signing a treaty to restrict such weapons was an indication of better relations.

In 1974 Nixon resigned from the presidency following the Watergate scandal. His successor was Gerald Ford, and his term would see the signing by thirty-five nations—including the superpowers—of the 1975 Helsinki Final Act. Two parts of this document pleased the Soviets: one confirmed the post–World War II European borders, and this recognized the communist status of Eastern Europe. In the spirit of détente, the other part encouraged trade, as well as cultural and scientific collaboration, among nations. The Soviets were less satisfied with the third part of the act, which related to human rights—the rights of all people that a government should not deny, from freedom of speech to freedom of religion. This part of the act guaranteed the free movement of people across borders and the free flow of ideas and information. The Soviets grudgingly signed the act but would fail to comply with its ideals. This issue would gain prominence as human rights groups in the West and dissidents—those who spoke against the government—and political prisoners in the Soviet Union called attention to the Soviet government's oppressive and sometimes abusive treatment of its people.

Jimmy Carter became president in 1976, and his administration would see the unraveling of détente. Americans were beginning to think that détente was making the nation weak and helping the Soviet Union grow stronger. In addition Carter placed a strong emphasis on human rights. The Soviets increasingly found themselves criticized for policies they felt were no one's business but their own. And when NATO decided to place American missiles in West Germany that could reach the USSR in six to twelve minutes, the Soviets were outraged. A second SALT agreement was signed in June 1979, but it was not enough to withstand the final blow to the era of détente: the Soviet invasion of Afghanistan in late December 1979.

Country Joe McDonald performing at the famous Woodstock Festival in upstate New York, 1969

What Are We Fighting For? Country Joe McDonald's Song of Protest

Throughout the Vietnam War, young poets and songwriters put their creativity to work to oppose violence, promote peace, and protest nuclear weapons. The following song, by Country Joe McDonald, was one of the most famous antiwar songs of the era.

I-FEEL-LIKE-I'M-FIXIN'-TO-DIE RAG

Yeah, come on all of you, big strong men.
Uncle Sam needs your help again.
He's got himself in a terrible jam.
Way down yonder in Vietnam.
So put down your books and pick up a gun.
We're gonna have a whole lotta fun.

Refrain:
And it's one, two, three,
What are we fightin' for?
Don't ask me, I don't give a damn.
Next stop is Vietnam;
And it's five, six, seven,
Open up the pearly gates,

Well, there ain't no time to wonder why,
Whoopee! we're all gonna die.

Huh! Well, come on Wall Street and don't be slow.
Why man this is war a-go-go.
There's plenty good money to be made,
By supplying the army with the tools of the trade.
Just hope and pray if they drop the bomb,
They drop it on the Vietcong.

(Refrain)

Well, come on Generals, let's move fast;
Your big chance has come at last.
Gotta go out and get those reds—

Wall Street
the financial center of the United States

Vietcong
communist forces in Vietnam

reds
Communists

The only good commie is one who's dead.
And you know that peace can only be won,
When we've blown 'em all to kingdom come.

(Refrain)

Well, come on mothers throughout the land,
Pack your boys off to Vietnam.
Come on fathers, don't hesitate,
Send 'em off before it's too late.
Be the first one on your block
To have your boy come home in a box.

(Refrain)

—From "I-Feel-Like-I'm-Fixin'-to-Die Rag," lyrics by Joe McDonald,
copyright © 1965, renewed 1993 by Alkatraz Corner Music.

THINK ABOUT THIS

1. Whom did McDonald blame for capitalizing on the Vietnam War?

2. Where does he indicate his opposition to the U.S. policy of containment of the spread of communism?

3. What effect do you think songs like this one had on young people during the Vietnam War?

4. How may the antiwar movement have influenced the U.S. move toward détente?

Nixon in China

The United States had been on rocky terms with the People's Republic of China since its birth as a communist nation in October of 1949. In fact, the United States refused to recognize Communist China and gave its support to Taiwan. It was to this island, off the Chinese mainland, that exiles opposed to communism had fled in 1949. Called the Republic of China, Taiwan had remained a capitalist society.

In February 1972 Richard Nixon became the first U.S. president to visit China. He is shown here with Chinese premier Chou En-lai at a banquet in Shanghai.

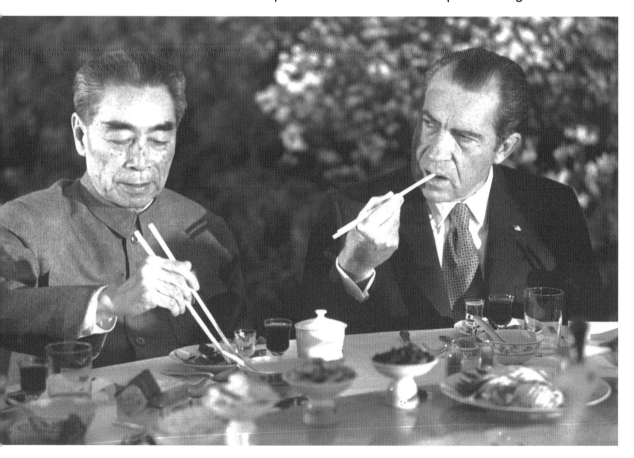

The war in Vietnam fueled the troubles, for the presence of U.S. troops on the Asian continent was disturbing to the Chinese. But by the end of the 1960s the United States was starting to withdraw troops from Vietnam. At the same time, tensions between China and the Soviet Union were at an all-time high. With a decreasing U.S. presence in Asia, the Chinese began to see the Soviets as the greater threat. President Richard Nixon and his national security adviser, Henry Kissinger, believed that by recognizing Red China they might be able to diminish Soviet power in the region. Chinese and U.S. officials began meeting in secret. It was a slow process, but by February 1972 relations had improved enough for Nixon to be the first American president to visit China. The following is a portion of the joint communiqué issued by the U.S. and Chinese governments, which detailed the events of this historic trip.

DURING THE VISIT, extensive, earnest and frank discussions were held between President Nixon and Premier Zhou Enlai on the normalization of relations between the United States of America and the People's Republic of China. . . .

The U.S. side stated: . . . The United States supports individual freedom and social progress for all the peoples of the world, free of outside pressure or intervention. The United States believes that the effort to reduce tensions is served by improving communication between countries that have different ideologies so as to lessen the risks of confrontation through accident, miscalculation or misunderstanding. . . .

The Chinese side stated: Wherever there is oppression, there is resistance. Countries want independence, nations want liberation and the people want revolution—this has become the irresistible trend of history. All nations, big or small, should be equal. . . . The Chinese side . . . firmly supports the struggles of all the oppressed people and nations for freedom and liberation and [believes] that the people of all countries have the right to choose their social systems according to their own wishes. . . .

There are essential differences between China and the United States in their social systems and foreign policies. However, the two sides agreed that countries, regardless of their social systems, should conduct their relations on the principles of respect for the sovereignty and territorial integrity of all states, non-aggression against other states, non-interference in the internal affairs of other states, equality and mutual benefit, and peaceful coexistence. International disputes should be settled on this basis, without resorting to the use or threat of force. . . .

"There are essential differences between China and the United States."

Both sides are of the view that it would be against the interests of the peoples of the world for any major country to collude with another against other countries, or for major countries to divide up the world into spheres of interest. . . .

The two sides expressed the hope that the gains achieved during this visit would open up new prospects for the relations between the two countries.

—*From the Joint Communiqué between the People's Republic of China and the United States of America, issued in Shanghai, February 27, 1972.*

1. Both the Chinese and the Americans said they favored freedom. As communist versus democratic governments, how might their definitions of freedom have differed?

2. Why do you think the two governments issued this communiqué? How do you think the Soviet Union reacted to it?

3. How does the communiqué suggest that countries with different ideologies can coexist?

Nixon in the USSR

The year 1972 was one of intense travel for President Nixon. In May, just months after his historic trip to China, he visited the Soviet Union with two goals in mind: to prevent nuclear war and to slow the arms race. The trip marked a historic moment in history, as Nixon and Soviet leader Leonid Brezhnev signed the SALT and the ABM treaties. After twenty-five years of conflict, the superpowers were seeking ways to coexist. Following is an excerpt of Nixon's speech to the people of the Soviet Union, which was broadcast on television and radio in both Russia and the United States.

FOR THE 3 YEARS I HAVE BEEN IN OFFICE, one of my principal aims has been to establish a better relationship between the United States and the Soviet Union. Our two countries have much in common. Most important of all, we have never fought one another in war. On the contrary, the memory of your soldiers and ours embracing at the Elbe, as allies, in 1945, remains strong in millions of hearts in both of our countries. It is my hope that that memory can serve as an inspiration for the renewal of Soviet-American cooperation in the 1970's.

As great powers, we shall sometimes be competitors, but we need never be enemies.

". . . there would be no winners, only losers."

In our meetings this week . . . we have taken an historic first step in the limitation of nuclear strategic arms. This arms control agreement is not for the purpose of giving either side an advantage over the other. Both of our nations are strong. . . . Each will maintain the strength necessary to defend its independence.

But in an unchecked arms race between two great nations, there would be no winners, only losers. By setting this limitation together, the people of both our nations, and of all nations, can be winners.

—*From the* Public Papers of President Richard Nixon, *1972.*
"Radio and Television Address to the People of the Soviet Union, May 28, 1972."
The Richard Nixon Library and Birthplace Foundation.

THINK ABOUT THIS

How do you think Soviet citizens reacted to this speech? Would American citizens have reacted differently?

The Cold War Renewed: Jimmy Carter's State of the Union Address

By the time Jimmy Carter gave his State of the Union address on January 21, 1980, the era of détente was over, and the United States stood at a critical juncture. The Soviets had invaded Afghanistan the month before, and the Cold War was still on. Carter would soon increase defense spending and remove his support from a new treaty, SALT II. The prospect of nuclear war loomed once again. Following are portions of Carter's State of the Union address.

[T]HE SOVIET UNION HAS TAKEN A RADICAL and an aggressive new step. It's using its great military power against a relatively defense-less nation. The implications of the Soviet invasion of Afghanistan could pose the most serious threat to the peace since the Second World War. . . .

While this invasion continues, we and the other nations of the world cannot conduct business as usual with the Soviet Union. That's why the United States has imposed stiff economic penalties on the Soviet Union. I will not issue any permits for Soviet ships to fish in the coastal waters of the United States. I've cut Soviet access to high-technology equipment and to agricultural products. I've limited other commerce with the Soviet Union, and I've asked our allies and friends to join with us in restraining their own trade with the Soviets and not to replace our own embargoed items. And I have notified the Olympic Committee that with Soviet invading forces in Afghanistan, neither the American people nor I will support sending an Olympic team to Moscow. . . .

The region which is now threatened by Soviet troops in Afghanistan is of great strategic importance: It contains more than

> *". . . such an assault will be repelled by any means necessary, including military force."*

two-thirds of the world's exportable oil. The Soviet effort to dominate Afghanistan has brought Soviet military forces to within 300 miles of the Indian Ocean and close to the Straits of Hormuz, a waterway through which most of the world's oil must flow. The Soviet Union is now attempting to consolidate a strategic position, therefore, that poses a grave threat to the free movement of Middle East oil. . . .

Let our position be absolutely clear: An attempt by any outside force to gain control of the Persian Gulf region will be regarded as an assault on the vital interests of the United States of America, and such an assault will be repelled by any means necessary, including military force.

—From President Jimmy Carter, "State of the Union Address 1980," delivered January 21, 1980. Available at the Jimmy Carter Library Web site: http://www.jimmycarterlibrary.org/documents/speeches/su80jec.phtml

THINK ABOUT THIS

1. In what ways did Carter choose to punish the Soviet Union for the invasion of Afghanistan?
2. Why was the region that the Soviets invaded so important to the United States?

Reagan Denounces an Evil Empire

Jimmy Carter lost the election in November 1980, in part because many Americans believed the United States had become weak under his watch. The new president was Ronald Reagan, who had harshly criticized détente during his campaign. Throughout his political career, Reagan had been an outspoken anti-Communist.

"The objective I propose is quite simple to state: to foster the infrastructure of democracy . . . , which allows a people to choose their own way to develop their own culture, to reconcile their own differences through peaceful means." —President Ronald Reagan, June 8, 1982.

When he became president, he made it clear that the era of détente was over; his would be a presidency of tough talk and firm negotiation. He branded the Soviet Union an "Evil Empire," a term that would long be remembered. He accused the Soviets of lying and cheating whenever such behavior served their purposes. Following are portions from three public speeches in his first years as president. They provided Americans, and people around the world, with a clear expression of the new president's convictions.

EXCERPT FROM PRESIDENT REAGAN'S FIRST PRESS CONFERENCE,
JANUARY 29, 1981—

Q. Mr. President, what do you see as the long-range intentions
of the Soviet Union? Do you think, for instance, the Kremlin is bent
on world domination that might lead to a continuation of the Cold
War? Or do you think that under other circumstances détente is
possible?

A. Well, so far détente's been a one-way street the Soviet Union
has used to pursue its own aims. I don't have to think of an answer
as to what I think their intentions are:
They have repeated it. I know of no leader
of the Soviet Union, since the [Bolshevik]
revolution and including the present leadership, that has not more than once
repeated in the various Communist con-
gresses they hold their determination that
their goal must be the promotion of world revolution and a one world
Socialist or Communist state, whichever word you want to use.

"Well, so far détente's been a one-way street."

Now, as long as they do that and as long as they, at the same time,
have openly and publicly declared that the only morality they recognize is what will further their cause, meaning they reserve unto themselves the right to commit any crime, to lie, to cheat . . . I think when
you do business with them, even at a détente, you keep that in mind.

FROM PRESIDENT REAGAN'S ADDRESS TO THE MEMBERS OF
THE BRITISH PARLIAMENT, JUNE 8, 1982—

. . . the regimes planted by totalitarianism have had more than
30 years to establish their legitimacy. But none—not one regime—
has yet been able to risk free elections. Regimes planted by bayonets
do not take root. . . .

Historians looking back at our time will note the consistent restraint and peaceful intentions of the West. They will note that it was the democracies who refused to use the threat of their nuclear monopoly in the forties and early fifties for territorial or imperial gain. Had that nuclear monopoly been in the hands of the Communist world, the map of Europe—indeed, the world—would look very different today. . . .

The objective I propose is quite simple to state: to foster the infrastructure of democracy, the system of a free press, unions, political parties, universities, which allows a people to choose their own way to develop their own culture, to reconcile their own differences through peaceful means.

Our military strength is a prerequisite to peace, but let it be clear we maintain this strength in the hope it will never be used, for the ultimate determinant in the struggle that's now going on in the world will not be bombs and rockets, but a test of wills and ideas, a trial of spiritual resolve, the values we hold, the beliefs we cherish, the ideals to which we are dedicated.

FROM PRESIDENT REAGAN'S SPEECH GIVEN MARCH 8, 1983,
IN ORLANDO, FLORIDA—

I intend to do everything I can to persuade them [the Soviets] of our peaceful intent, to remind them that it was the West that refused to use its nuclear monopoly in the forties and fifties for territorial gain and which now proposes fifty percent cuts in strategic ballistic missiles and the elimination of an entire class of land-based intermediate-range nuclear missiles [those that could travel 300 to 3,400 miles (500 to 5,500 kilometers)].

At the same time, however, they must be made to understand we will never compromise our principles and standards. We will never give away our freedom. We will never abandon our belief in God. And we will never stop searching for a genuine peace. But we can assure none of these things America stands for through the so-called nuclear freeze solutions proposed by some. . . . The reality is we must find peace through strength.

Let us pray for the salvation of all those who live in totalitarian darkness, pray they will discover the joy of knowing God. But until they do, let us be aware that while they preach the supremacy of the state, declare its omnipotence over individual man, and predict its eventual domination of all peoples on earth—they are the focus of evil in the modern world.

—*From* The Public Papers of President Ronald W. Reagan, *Ronald Reagan Presidential Foundation and Library, Simi Valley, California.*

THINK ABOUT THIS

1. What common themes run through these speeches?
2. What does Reagan suggest would have happened if the Soviets had achieved nuclear capability before the United States?
3. What distinctions did Reagan draw between communist and democratic governments?
4. Can you draw any connections between Reagan's views and those of the George W. Bush administration?

The infamous "witch hunts" of Senator Joseph McCarthy *(right)* during the 1950s sought to root out Communist infiltrators within the United States. These investigations ruined the careers and lives of numerous people, yet Senator McCarthy characterized his activities as a "moral uprising" that would "end only when the whole sorry mess of twisted warped thinkers are swept from the national scene."

Chapter 6

Homeland Hysteria

FOR MOST OF THE COLD WAR, Americans had a sense of great unease: at any moment, the Soviets could drop the bomb. This inflamed a variety of fears. Some people sought to uncover Communists in the United States, who, they believed, might try to help the Soviets. Others were on the lookout for spies, both legitimate and falsely accused. Still others built elaborate private bomb shelters where they could hide with their families in the event of nuclear attack. Radio and television announcements warned of impending doom. A propaganda film in the early 1960s, for example, sent out the following chilling message: "And by the way, do you know exactly what your family would do if an attack came, say at 10 o'clock tomorrow morning? Good question, isn't it?"

During World War II, Americans and Soviets had set aside their differences as they became allies in the fight against Nazi Germany. But the old fears and suspicions that existed from the 1917 Bolshevik Revolution forward were quickly rekindled after the war. The House Un-American Activities Committee (HUAC), established in 1938, was a congressional committee charged with uncovering subversive—or un-American—activities in the government. Initially its job was to root out possible traitors who might pass on information to the Nazis, the Japanese, or other unfriendly forces. But after the war, the concern was much different. The committee began looking for "Reds"—Communists—living in the United States. In the fall of 1947 HUAC began an investigation of Hollywood writers, producers, and performers to determine whether Communists had infiltrated the entertainment industry. Many were called to testify before Congress, and most cooperated. But a small group refused to answer questions about their political affiliation, claiming rights under the First Amendment. This group, known as the Hollywood Ten, were jailed for four to ten months for their refusal to testify. Once out of jail, they were blacklisted by the film industry; none of the Hollywood Ten could find a job without leaving the country or using a false name.

This was just the beginning of an era of paranoia and suspicion, led largely by a senator named Joseph McCarthy and the head of the Federal Bureau of Investigation, J. Edgar Hoover. McCarthy stirred up anti-Communist furor by claiming there were "Reds" working in important government positions, putting national security at risk. The investigations he sponsored came to be called witch hunts, and they affected people from every walk of life, not just government employees. With a simple accusation, people could lose their reputations and their livelihoods. McCarthy became so obsessed with hunting down Communists that the term *McCarthyism* has come into the language to describe such indiscriminate attacks on people. For his part, Hoover allowed his FBI agents to use any tactic—from break-ins to bugging to telephone eavesdropping—to uncover Communists plotting in America. He encouraged neighbors to spy on each other, friends to report suspicious activities, and even children to inform on their parents.

The fear surrounding the "Red Menace" may have been exaggerated, but there was real reason for concern. The KGB, the Soviet agency in charge of intelligence, was tremendously skilled at espionage, or spying. The Soviets were also skilled at recruiting Americans and other Westerners to pass information to them. In January of 1950 a German-born scientist named Klaus Fuchs was arrested in London. He had worked at the U.S. Atomic Research Laboratory in New Mexico during the top-secret Manhattan Project. Fuchs admitted to passing secrets about the bomb to the Soviets, which helped them build their own all the more quickly. He also turned over the names of several Americans who had done the same, including Julius and Ethel Rosenberg. Fuchs, Julius Rosenberg, and others in their network believed it was wrong for a single country—the United States—to possess such enormous power. But their actions were considered treasonous. In this chapter, you'll get a sense of what it was like to live in the era of McCarthyism, when the Red Scare was at its height.

The Alger Hiss Case

In 1948 a former Communist named Whittaker Chambers appeared before the House Un-American Activities Committee and gave the names of government employees who were members of the Communist Party. Among them was Alger Hiss, who had been an important aide to Democratic president Franklin

A young congressman named Richard Nixon *(right)* took advantage of the "Red Scare" to further his political career during the Alger Hiss affair.

D. Roosevelt. Chambers claimed that Hiss was not only a member of the Communist Party, but a secret agent as well. Hiss proclaimed his innocence in testimony before HUAC. One member of the committee didn't believe him: Richard Nixon, then a first-term Republican congressman. Convinced Hiss was lying, Nixon doggedly questioned him before a congressional hearing, but Hiss would admit to nothing. When Hiss sued Chambers for libel, Chambers produced sixty-five typed pages that he claimed proved Hiss's guilt. He said Hiss had typed these documents, then given them to Chambers to turn over to the Soviets. Unable to prove he hadn't, Hiss was found guilty of perjury, or lying under oath, about his involvement in Communist activities. He served forty-four months in prison but always maintained his innocence until his death in 1996 at age ninety-two. Over the years, increasing evidence has mounted in support of Hiss's claim, but many still question his innocence. Following is his recollection of the McCarthy era. Hiss wrote this article in 1980 when, as the Cold War was regaining momentum, people wondered if the witch hunts of the 1950s could happen again.

IT IS DIFFICULT BUT NECESSARY for young people, not only students, but most Americans under forty, to grasp the extent and fury of the hysteria that gripped the country from the late '40s until the mid-'50s. All over the country, thousands of Americans entered into a nightmare world of inquisition—by Congressional and state legislative committees, FBI agents, and local vigilantes, all of whom publicly sought to point the finger at "subversives."

Many thousands of teachers, office workers, seamen, union members, government employees, editors, social workers, actors, lawyers, accountants, radio and TV entertainers, writers—people in every walk of life, the obscure and the prominent—were publicly attacked, driven from their jobs, and ostracized by neighbors and fair-weather friends. As David Caute pointed out, these victims of the McCarthyite purges were guilty of "no crime worse than the opinions they held, or had once held" (*New Statesman,* December 16, 1977). The extent of human injury was, of course, not limited to those pilloried or purged; their wives, husbands, children, other relatives and close associates add additional thousands to the list.

More importantly, the nation was deprived for years to come of

". . . the nation was deprived . . . of the independent thought and initiative of many citizens."

the independent thought and initiative of many citizens who were either cowed by the fates of the victims or simply wanted "to avoid trouble."

—From Alger Hiss, "The McCarthy Period," Barrister, *1980. To read the entire article, visit http://homepages.nyu.edu/~th15/barristr.html*

Think about This

Hiss said that the anti-Communist witch hunts deprived the nation of "independent thought." What did he mean by this?

A Witness Describes the Rosenberg Execution

In 1950 a series of arrests led FBI investigators to a young electrical engineer named Julius Rosenberg, whom they accused of passing atomic secrets to the Soviets. After his arrest, FBI authorities assumed Rosenberg would supply the names of more spies from his network, but he refused. Although the case against his wife, Ethel, was weak, J. Edgar Hoover believed that threatening her with prosecution would make Julius talk. Ethel Rosenberg was arrested and taken to jail, yet Julius remained silent. With evidence provided by two other spies, the Rosenbergs were found guilty and sentenced to the electric chair. The severe punishment reflected both the strong anti-Communist sentiment of the day and a government strategy to get Julius Rosenberg to confess in hopes of avoiding execution. People all over the world protested the sentence; many claimed both were innocent. Both Albert

Einstein and Pope Pius XII asked that the Rosenbergs' lives be spared. Despite the pleas on their behalf, the Rosenbergs were executed on June 19, 1953. Today, evidence from a Soviet KGB agent indicates that Julius was guilty of espionage. But Ethel's guilt is still in question. It may be that she knew of her husband's activities but was not involved herself. The story of the Rosenbergs remains controversial even now. Following is the testimony of a witness who was present at the execution.

Julius and Ethel Rosenberg during their espionage trial. Even today many people still question the couple's guilt, although evidence suggests that Julius was indeed a spy.

HE DIED QUICKLY, there didn't seem to be too much life left in him when he entered behind the rabbi. He seemed to be walking in a cadence of steps as if keeping in time with the muttering of the 23rd Psalm. She died a lot harder. When it appeared that she had received enough electricity to kill an ordinary person and had received the exact amount that had killed her husband, the doctors went over and pulled down the cheap prison dress, a little dark green printed job, and placed the steto . . . stetho . . . can't say it . . . placed the stethoscopes to her and then looked around and looked at each other

The Rosenberg execution was a controversial issue, but many Americans could hardly be said to have felt sorry for the couple.

rather dumbfounded and seemed surprised that she was not dead. And she was given more electricity which started again and a kind of a ghastly plume of smoke rose from her head and went up against the skylight overhead. After two more of those jolts, Ethel Rosenberg had met her maker. She'll have a lot of explaining to do too. Thank you.

—From archival footage, witness to Rosenberg execution, available at http://www.cnn.com/SPECIALS/cold.war/ episodes/06/script.html

THINK ABOUT THIS

1. Did the witness sympathize with the Rosenbergs?
2. Do you think the death penalty was an appropriate punishment for this crime, since Julius Rosenberg's actions may have resulted in the Soviets' obtaining an atomic bomb?

McCarthy on Communists

In 1949 the Soviets had just detonated their first bomb, and China had proclaimed itself Communist. Many Americans feared the nation was losing ground against communism and wondered what had become of the country that had fought so valiantly in World War II. It was in this anxious climate that Joseph McCarthy, a first-term Republican senator, began to present himself as a public crusader against the Communist threat in the United States, cooperating with House leaders on HUAC. As Nixon had before him, McCarthy recognized the Red Scare as a means to further his own career, and to criticize the Democratic Party for being soft on communism. He began publicly accusing a wide variety of people—from government officials to playwrights, performers, and professors—of being disloyal to the United States. Some of these people had ties to leftist organizations, but that did not make them traitors. Once accused, most could do nothing to save their ruined reputations. They faced loss of employment, damaged careers, and ruined lives. The speech that follows provides a glimpse of McCarthy's tactics.

TODAY WE ARE ENGAGED in a final, all-out battle between communistic atheism and Christianity. The modern champions of communism have selected this as the time. And, ladies and gentlemen, the chips are down—they are truly down. . . .

Six years ago . . . there was within the Soviet orbit 180,000,000 people. . . . Today, only 6 years later, there are 800,000,000 people under the absolute domination of Soviet Russia—an increase of over 400 percent. On our side, the figure has shrunk to around

500,000,000. In other words, in less than 6 years the odds have changed from 9 to 1 in our favor to 8 to 5 against us. This indicates the swiftness of the tempo of Communist victories and American defeats in the cold war. As one of our outstanding historical figures once said, "When a great democracy is destroyed, it will not be because of enemies from without, but rather because of enemies from within." The truth of this statement is becoming terrifyingly clear as we see this country each day losing on every front. . . .

The reason why we find ourselves in a position of impotency is not because our only powerful potential enemy has sent men to invade our shores, but rather because of the traitorous actions of those who have been treated so well by this Nation. . . .

". . . the State Department . . . is thoroughly infested with Communists."

This is glaringly true in the State Department. . . . In my opinion the State Department, which is one of the most important government departments, is thoroughly infested with Communists.

I have in my hand 57 cases of individuals who would appear to be either card carrying members or certainly loyal to the Communist Party, but who nevertheless are still helping to shape our foreign policy.

—*From a speech read by Senator Joseph McCarthy to the U.S. Senate.* Congressional Record of the Senate, *81st Congress 2nd Session, February 20, 1950. 1954–1957.*

THINK ABOUT THIS

1. How did McCarthy describe the current world situation? What evidence did he provide?

2. Why do you think many Americans, including members of Congress, believed McCarthy's accusations?

McCarthy continued his anti-communism crusade until 1954, when he finally went too far. He accused members of the U.S. Army of disloyalty, and the hearings appeared on television. The whole world watched as McCarthy accused a young man of subversive activities and was then proven wrong. Few people had the courage to stand up to McCarthy, but a Boston lawyer named Joseph Welch did. "Have you no sense of decency, sir, at long last?" he asked. "Have you left no sense of decency?" This was not the first time that McCarthy was criticized for his tactics. In 1950 Republican Margaret Chase Smith was the first senator to denounce him as she presented her "Declaration of Conscience" on the Senate floor. Smith was staunchly anti-Communist, but she knew that McCarthy's actions were unjust.

In chastising McCarthy, Margaret Chase Smith spoke out against a member of her own political party. Smith served in the U.S. Senate from 1949 until 1973.

THOSE OF US WHO SHOUT THE LOUDEST about Americanism in making character assassinations are all too frequently those who, by our own words and acts, ignore some of the basic principles of Americanism—the right to criticize; the right to hold unpopular beliefs; the right to protest; the right of independent thought.

The exercise of these rights should not cost one single American citizen his reputation or his right to a livelihood nor should he be in danger of losing his reputation or livelihood merely because he happens to know someone who holds unpopular beliefs. Who of us doesn't? Otherwise none of us could call our souls our own. Otherwise thought control would have set in.

"Freedom of speech is not what it used to be in America."

The American people are sick and tired of being afraid to speak their minds lest they be politically smeared as "Communists". . . . Freedom of speech is not what it used to be in America. It has been so abused by some that it is not exercised by others. . . .

As a United States Senator, I am not proud of the way in which the Senate has been made a publicity platform for irresponsible sensationalism. I am not proud of the reckless abandon in which unproved charges have been hurled from this side of the aisle [from Republicans on the Senate floor]. I am not proud of the obviously staged, undignified countercharges that have been attempted in retaliation from the other side of the aisle [from Democrats on the Senate floor].

I don't like the way the Senate has been made a rendezvous for vilification, for selfish political gain at the sacrifice of individual reputations and national unity. I am not proud of the way we smear outsiders from the floor of the Senate and hide behind the cloak of congressional immunity and still place ourselves beyond criticism on the floor of the Senate.

—*From Senator Margaret Chase Smith, "Declaration of Conscience," address to the Senate*. Congressional Record of the Senate, *82nd Congress, 1st Session, June 1, 1950*.

THINK ABOUT THIS

1. According to Smith, how might McCarthy himself be considered "un-American"?
2. What did Smith mean when she said freedom of speech "has been so abused by some that it is not exercised by others"?
3. Why was Smith critical of the Senate?

Be Prepared: The Office of Civil Defense Warns Americans

During World War II the Department of Defense established the Office of Civil Defense (OCD), whose job was to find ways to protect the public in the event of an emergency. With new fears ignited by the Cold War, Soviet attack became the new concern of the OCD. The agency produced numerous public announcements to prepare Americans in case of attack, sometimes with the result of frightening people all the more.

A RADIO SPOT EXPLAINS WHAT FALLOUT IS—
This is basic civil defense information from the Department of Defense, Office of Civil Defense, Washington. When a nuclear bomb or missile explodes near the ground, great quantities of earth and debris are sucked up into the fireball and carried by the prevailing winds before

falling back to Earth. This material is radioactive fallout. The particles look like grains of salt or sand. Fallout gives off invisible gamma rays, like X-rays, and heavy exposure to it can cause serious radiation sickness—even death. If a person receives a small or medium dose of radiation, his body will repair itself, and he will get well. Usually the effects of radiation from fallout are more severe in very young and very old persons and those not in good health. Radiation sickness is not contagious. The most dangerous period is the first twenty-four hours after fallout arrives. But you might have to use a fallout shelter up to two weeks. For further information about fallout and how you can protect yourself against it, consult your local civil defense office.

> *". . . heavy exposure to it can cause serious radiation sickness—even death."*

—From "In Time of Emergency Radio Kit No. 1," Department of Defense, Office of Civil Defense, 1968.

AN OFFICE OF CIVIL DEFENSE BROCHURE OFFERS THE FOLLOWING ADVICE ABOUT HOW TO STOCK A FALLOUT SHELTER—

Before Disaster Strikes You Should Have on Hand:

1. Flashlight and extra batteries.
2. Battery-powered portable radio and extra batteries.
3. First-aid kits.
4. Stored water or other liquid—7 gallons per person for 2 weeks. . . .
5. A 14-day supply of food. . . .
6. Cooking and eating utensils. . . .
7. Special foods for babies and invalids.
8. Large garbage can (20 gallons).

Many Americans built underground bomb shelters like this one in response to the high anxiety the Cold War produced.

9. Smaller can for human wastes (10 gallons).

10. Covered pail for bathroom purposes.

11. Toilet tissue, paper towels, personal sanitary supplies, disposable diapers, and soap.

12. One blanket per person. . . .

13. Grocery bags and a week's accumulation of newspapers for wrapping garbage.

14. Two pints of household chlorine, and 1 quart of 5 percent DDT [a pesticide].

15. Wrench, screwdriver, and shovel; axe and crowbar to free yourself from debris . . . [and] to help others. . . .

16. Waterproof gloves.

—From "Ten for Survival. Survive a Nuclear Attack." Office of Civil Defense and Mobilization, May 1959 (reprinted March 1961).

THINK ABOUT THIS

1. How do you think people felt when they heard Civil Defense radio announcements like the one featured here?

2. Can you think of situations today that would drive people to make similar preparations for survival?

Chapter 7

Ban the Bomb:
Peace Activists Speak Out

NOT LONG AFTER THE WORLD LEARNED about the bombing of Hiroshima, people began to speak out against the destructive potential of nuclear weapons. On the day Nagasaki was bombed, British mathematician and philosopher Bertrand Russell wrote the following: "It is impossible to imagine a more dramatic and horrifying combination of scientific triumph with political and moral failure than has been shown to the world in the destruction of Hiroshima. . . . As I write, I learn that a second bomb has been dropped on Nagasaki. The prospect for the human race is somber beyond all precedent. Mankind are faced with a clear-cut alternative: either we shall all perish, or we shall have to acquire some slight degree of common sense." Russell would go on to found one of the first "ban the bomb" organizations, the Campaign for Nuclear Disarmament, and the Pugwash Conferences, a forum for scientists seeking to promote peace. He also inspired a generation of antiwar and antinuclear protesters.

Public protests were taking place by the 1950s, first in Europe and later in the United States. Scientists began to warn of the

During the Cold War, women were among the most vocal critics of nuclear defense, but people from all walks of life had reason to fear and protest the deadly technology. Over the years, increasing numbers of people around the world, like these protestors in England, would join in the call for nuclear disarmament.

dangers of continuing the arms race. In 1956 the nuclear issue became a focus of national politics. The Democratic presidential candidate, Adlai Stevenson, was running against President Eisenhower. Stevenson proposed a halt to testing of the H-bomb and challenged other nations to do the same, saying "there is not peace—real peace—while more than half of our federal budget goes into an armaments race . . . and the earth's atmosphere is contaminated from week to week by exploding hydrogen bombs." Stevenson's words were daring, given the climate of the time, in which the nation was terrified of the possibility of nuclear attack. Republicans sharply disagreed with Stevenson; nuclear weapons were at the center of President Eisenhower's national security policy. Vice President Nixon called Stevenson's ideas "catastrophic nonsense." But Stevenson pressed on, saying a ban on nuclear testing would be a first priority if he were elected. His ideas garnered much support, including that of leading scientists. But when the Soviets praised Stevenson's ideas, the public began to worry. Would a ban on testing and an easing of the arms race leave America vulnerable? Ultimately, Eisenhower would be elected to another term as president.

The concern about nuclear arms did not go away. In 1957 the Committee for a Sane Nuclear Policy (SANE), an organization of private citizens seeking to alter official nuclear policies, was formed. Similar organizations would appear throughout the Cold War. In the nearly fifty years of the Cold War, there were always people who spoke out against nuclear weapons, who dreamed of world peace. Some of these activists were famous, others not. Some were writers and artists, others ordinary people. Some spoke to world leaders, others to scientists, and others to the public. But all of these activists had a common goal: to warn people of the danger that lay ahead if the arms race did not come to an end.

A Manifesto: Einstein and Russell Send a Warning

In 1939 the brilliant physicist Albert Einstein, who was born in Germany but later became a U.S. citizen, had called Franklin Roosevelt's attention to the potential of atomic energy. He warned the president to make every effort to ensure that the United States tapped into its destructive power before the Germans did so. His advice led to the Manhattan Project—and ultimately to the first atomic bomb. Ten years after the bombing of Hiroshima, Einstein and Bertrand Russell released a manifesto, or public declaration, warning of the dangers of nuclear weapons and encouraging scientists to speak out against them. Highlights of their manifesto follow.

WE ARE SPEAKING ON THIS OCCASION, not as members of this or that nation, continent, or creed, but as human beings, members of the species Man, whose continued existence is in doubt. The world is full of conflicts; and, overshadowing all minor conflicts, the titanic struggle between Communism and anti-Communism.

Almost everybody who is politically conscious has strong feelings about one or more of these issues; but we want you, if you can, to set aside such feelings and consider yourselves only as members of a biological species which has had a remarkable history, and whose disappearance none of us can desire.

Albert Einstein *(top)* and Bertrand Russell issued their manifesto in July of 1955.

We shall try to say no single word which should appeal to one group rather than to another. All, equally, are in peril, and, if the peril is understood, there is hope that they may collectively avert it.

We have to learn to think in a new way. We have to learn to ask ourselves, not what steps can be taken to give military victory to whatever group we prefer, for there no longer are such steps; the question we have to ask ourselves is: what steps can be taken to prevent a military contest of which the issue must be disastrous to all parties?

The general public, and even many men in positions of authority, have not realized what would be involved in a war with nuclear bombs. The general public still thinks in terms of the obliteration of cities. It is understood that the new bombs are more powerful than the old, and that, while one A-bomb could obliterate Hiroshima, one H-bomb could obliterate the largest cities, such as London, New York, and Moscow.

No doubt in an H-bomb war great cities would be obliterated. But this is one of the minor disasters that would have to be faced. If everybody in London, New York, and Moscow were exterminated, the world might, in the course of a few centuries, recover from the blow. But we now know . . . that nuclear bombs can gradually spread destruction over a very much wider area than had been supposed.

It is stated on very good authority that a bomb can now be manufactured which will be 2,500 times as powerful as that which destroyed Hiroshima. . . . the best authorities are unanimous in saying that a war with H-bombs might possibly put an end to the human race. It is feared that if many H-bombs are used there will be universal death, sudden only for a minority, but for the majority a slow torture of disease and disintegration. . . .

"Shall we put an end to the human race; or shall mankind renounce war?"

Here, then, is the problem which we present to you, stark and dreadful and inescapable: Shall we put an end to the human race; or shall mankind renounce war? . . .

There lies before us, if we choose, continual progress in happiness, knowledge, and wisdom. Shall we, instead, choose death, because we cannot forget our quarrels? We appeal as human beings to human beings: Remember your humanity, and forget the rest. If you can do so, the way lies open to a new Paradise; if you cannot, there lies before you the risk of universal death.

—From *"The Russell-Einstein Manifesto," issued in London, 9 July 1955. For the full text, see http://www.pugwash.org/about/manifesto.htm*

THINK ABOUT THIS

1. What did Russell and Einstein ask readers of the manifesto to do as they reviewed the document? Why?

2. Would you have agreed with the message of the manifesto, or would you have supported Eisenhower's policy?

3. According to the authors, were most people aware of the degree of devastation nuclear war would cause?

A Satirist's Perspective: "We Will All Go Together"

Some people took a less serious approach to the nuclear debate. The following lyrics are by the humorous songwriter and college mathematics professor Tom Lehrer. He used satire to express his feelings about the perils of nuclear war. These are the first stanzas of his song "We Will All Go Together When We Go."

WE WILL ALL GO TOGETHER WHEN WE GO

When you attend a funeral,
It is sad to think that sooner o' later
Those you love will do the same for you.
And you may have thought it tragic,
Not to mention other adjectives,
To think of all the weeping they will do.
(But don't you worry.)
No more ashes, no more sackcloth,
And an armband made of black cloth
Will someday never more adorn a sleeve.
For if the Bomb that drops on you,
Gets your friends and neighbors too,
There'll be nobody left behind to grieve.

And we will all go together when we go,
What a comforting fact that is to know.
Universal bereavement,
An inspiring achievement,
Yes, we all will go together when we go.
We will all go together when we go,

All suffused in an incandescent glow,
No one will have the endurance
To collect on his insurance,
Lloyd's of London will be loaded when they go! . . .

And we will all go together when we go,
Every Hottentot and every Eskimo,
When the air becomes uranious,
We will all go simultaneous,
And we'll all go together
When we all go together,
Yes we all will go together when we go.

Lloyd's of London
an insurance firm

—*From "We Will All Go Together When We Go," copyright © 1958 by Tom Lehrer.*

American Women March for Peace

Over the years, women have been among the most outspoken of antinuclear activists, seeking a more peaceful world for themselves and their families. In 1979, following an accident at the Three Mile Island nuclear power plant in Pennsylvania, a group of women decided to march on the Pentagon, the headquarters of the nation's military. Some 2,500 women participated in the march, which took place on November 16, 1980. The group became known as the Women's Pentagon Action. Following is their "Unity Statement."

WE ARE GATHERING at the Pentagon on November 16 because we fear for our lives . . . the lives of this planet, our Earth, and the lives of the children who are our human future. . . . We want an end to the arms race. No more bombs. No more amazing inventions for death. . . .

Every day while we work, study, love, the colonels and generals who are planning our annihilation walk calmly in and out of its five sides [the five-sided Pentagon building]. They have accumulated over 30,000 nuclear bombs at the rate of three to six bombs a day. They are determined to produce the billion dollar MX missile. They are creating a technology called Stealth—the invisible, unperceivable arsenal. . . . We are in the hands of men whose power and wealth have separated them from the reality of daily life and the imagination. We have the right to be afraid.

> *"No more bombs. No more amazing inventions for death."*

—From *"The Women's Pentagon Action Unity Statement."* *In Patricia Cormack, editor,* Manifestos and Declarations of the Twentieth Century. *Toronto: Garamond, 1992.*

A Young Activist: Samantha Smith Writes to Andropov

Ten-year-old Samantha Smith of Manchester, Maine, worried that there might be a nuclear war one day. Leaders on both sides promised that they wouldn't be the first to start a war, she reasoned; then why were both sides stockpiling nuclear weapons? In 1982 Samantha suggested that her mother write a letter to the new Soviet leader, Yuri Andropov. Mrs. Smith suggested that Samantha write the letter instead, and that's exactly what she did. Andropov

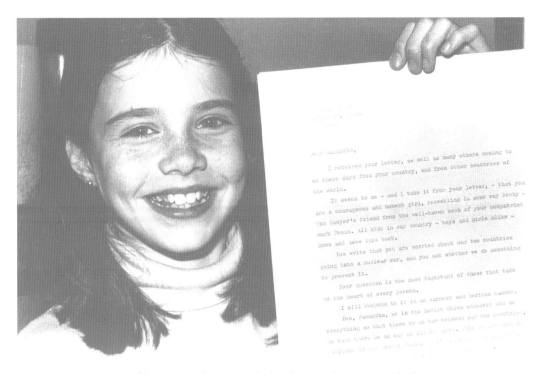

Samantha Smith holds a translation of the letter she received from Yuri Andropov. The text of this letter varies slightly from the one reproduced on the following pages. Different translators will often select different words or phrases to translate the same document.

did not respond immediately, but some months later a letter was waiting for Samantha. Not only did Andropov respond, he invited her to visit the Soviet Union. In July 1983 Samantha and her parents left for a two-week trip to the Soviet Union. While there, she stayed at a summer camp with children her own age. She laughed, talked, and learned folk songs, and through it all, she found that Russian children were not very different from kids in America. Samantha returned to the United States and wrote a book about her experience, *Journey to the Soviet Union.* She became recognized as an ambassador of world peace. She had the opportunity to travel and tell people about her experiences. Tragically, however,

Samantha's promising life was cut short. In 1985 she and her father were killed in an airplane crash. But her memory lived on, both at home and in the Soviet Union, where a stamp was issued in her honor. Samantha's letter, followed by Andropov's response, appears below.

Dear Mr. Andropov,

My name is Samantha Smith. I am ten years old. Congratulations on your new job. I have been worrying about Russia and the United States getting into a nuclear war. Are you going to vote to have a war or not? If you aren't please tell me how you are going to help to not have a war. This question you do not have to answer, but I would like to know why you want to conquer the world or at least our country. God made the world for us to live together in peace and not to fight.

> "I have been worrying about Russia and the United States getting into a nuclear war."

Sincerely,
Samantha Smith
Manchester, Maine USA

Dear Samantha,

I received your letter, which is like many others that have reached me recently from your country and from other countries around the world.

It seems to me—I can tell by your letter—that you are a courageous and honest girl, resembling Becky, the friend of Tom Sawyer in the famous book of your compatriot Mark Twain. This book is well known and loved in our country by all boys and girls.

You write that you are anxious about whether there will be a nuclear war between our two countries. And you ask are we doing anything so that war will not break out.

Your question is the most important of those that every thinking man can pose. I will reply to you seriously and honestly.

Yes, Samantha, we in the Soviet Union are trying to do everything so that there will not be war between our countries, so that in general there will not be war on earth. This is what every Soviet man wants. This is what the great founder of our state, Vladimir Lenin, taught us.

Soviet people well know what a terrible thing war is. Forty-two years ago, Nazi Germany, which strived for supremacy over the whole world, attacked our country, burned and destroyed many thousands of our towns and villages, killed millions of Soviet men, women and children.

In that war, which ended with our victory, we were in alliance with the United States: together we fought for the liberation of many people from the Nazi invaders. I hope that you know about this from your history lessons in school. And today we want very much to live in peace, to trade and cooperate with all our neighbors on this earth—with those far away and those near by. And certainly with such a great country as the United States of America.

In America and in our country there are nuclear weapons—terrible weapons that can kill millions of people in an instant. But we do not want them ever to be used. That's precisely why the Soviet Union solemnly declared throughout the entire world that never—never— will it use nuclear weapons first against any country. In general we propose to discontinue further production of them and to proceed to the abolition of all the stockpiles on earth.

It seems to me that this is a sufficient answer to your second question: "Why do you want to wage war against the whole world or at least the United States?" We want nothing of the kind. No one in our country—neither workers, peasants, writers nor doctors, neither grown-ups nor children, nor members of the government—wants either a big or "little" war.

We want peace—there is something that we are occupied with: growing wheat, building and inventing, writing books and flying into space. We want peace for ourselves and for all peoples of the planet. For our children and for you, Samantha.

I invite you, if your parents will let you, to come to our country, the best time being this summer. You will find out about our country, meet with your contemporaries, visit an international children's camp—"Artek"—on the sea. And see for yourself: in the Soviet Union—everyone is for peace and friendship among peoples.

Thank you for your letter. I wish you all the best in your young life.

Y. Andropov

—From Samantha Smith, Journey to the Soviet Union. *Boston: Little, Brown & Company, 1985, pp. 4, 6–9.*

THINK ABOUT THIS

1. Why do you think Andropov chose to respond to Samantha's letter?

2. People all over the world heard about Samantha's story. What effect do you think it might have had?

A Physician Speaks Out: Dr. Helen Caldicott

In the 1970s an Australian pediatrician, Dr. Helen Caldicott, became increasingly concerned about nuclear technology. At that time the French were conducting weapons tests in the South Pacific. When radioactive fallout from the tests was detected in her hometown of Adelaide, she began writing articles and giving speeches about the dangers of nuclear science. Soon she became well known for her direct—and alarming—talk about what would

Physician and peace activist Helen Caldicott presented a powerful argument against nuclear weapons, one that was frightening and all too real.

happen in the event of a nuclear war. In the late 1970s she moved to Boston, Massachusetts, to teach in the medical school at Harvard University. There she became the cofounder of Physicians for Social Responsibility and later the Women's Action for Nuclear Disarmament. Over the years she has been one of the most prominent voices of antinuclear activism. Following is a portion of a 1984 interview in which Caldicott described what would happen if a nuclear bomb were dropped. Her passionate voice inspired many others during the Cold War to become activists.

NUCLEAR WAR WILL CREATE THE FINAL MEDICAL EPIDEMIC of the human race, not just the human race, but all the plants and the animals. At risk right now is billions of years of evolution and creation, and we, you and I, hold it in the palm of our hands. And we will decide in our lifetime whether or not that continues to exist. . . .

[CALDICOTT DESCRIBES WHAT WOULD HAPPEN IF A 20-MEGATON BOMB WERE DROPPED ON A CITY.]

It will come in at 20 times the speed of sound . . . and explode in the fraction of a millionth of a second with the heat of the sun. And dig a hole three-quarters of a mile wide and 800 feet deep. . . . Six miles from the epicenter, every building will be flattened, concrete and steel will melt, and everyone will be killed, most people being vaporized, because 80% of our body is made of water, and as happened in Hiroshima, when we're exposed to the heat of the sun, we turn into gas and we disappear. Twenty miles from the epicenter, everyone [is] killed or lethally injured. Winds of 500 miles an hour just pick people up and turn them into missiles traveling at 100 miles an hour. The overpressures popcorn the windows and then shards of glass flying at 100 miles an hour will decapitate people and enter human flesh. People . . . who look at the flash, their eyes will melt. . . . Others will be charcoalized—turned into charcoal statues. All will be hideously burnt. Some will die immediately, some will die over days in the most intense agony, having never seen a physician for their pain. . . .

"Nuclear war will create the final medical epidemic of the human race."

We were here for three million years and lived symbiotically with nature, and now we've learned how to destroy it. The question is, we're at a crossroads of time now; can we evolve spiritually and emotionally fast enough to catch up to what the technology has produced in the world so that we can stop ourselves being destroyed? That's the question of our time. . . . If we die of natural causes, we'll know that we succeeded in that spiritual and emotional growth. If we die in a thermonuclear holocaust in the next four to ten years, we'll know we failed.

—From "The Urgency of the Nuclear Threat," interview with Dr. Helen Caldicott by John M. Whiteley. Quest for Peace video series, 1984.

THINK ABOUT THIS

1. Why did Caldicott call nuclear war the "final medical epidemic"?

2. Why do you think she had a strong effect on people who heard her speak?

Ronald Reagan and the new Soviet leader, Mikhail Gorbachev, hit it off well.
Although at times strained, their relationship would prove instrumental in
bringing the Cold War to its conclusion.

Chapter 8

End in Sight: The Conclusion of the Cold War

WHEN RONALD REAGAN TOOK the oath of office in January 1981, it was difficult to believe the Cold War would ever end. By then it had been raging for nearly forty years. As Reagan stepped up his hard-line approach to dealing with Communists, those who sought peace through disarmament thought their goals would never be reached. The 1980s would prove to be a decade of renewed fear, but also one in which relations between the two nations would thaw to an unexpected degree. This was the decade that would see the end of the nation's longest war.

At the dawn of the 1980s, the economy of the USSR was in dire straits. The Soviet people led dreary and difficult lives. Four families often lived in a single apartment. People waited in line for hours to purchase basic necessities. And despite the huge sums of money that were poured into the defense budget, the nation lagged behind the United States in the arms race.

Soviet leaders needed to find a way to renew the era of détente and negotiation, but Washington was unwilling to compromise.

Convinced the United States had grown too weak, Reagan would not promote arms control. Instead he suggested a new way to ensure the nation's security—a defensive system known as the Strategic Defense Initiative (SDI), a proposal for an antimissile shield stationed in space that would locate and destroy any missile before it could strike the United States. The SDI project soon became known as Star Wars. Reagan claimed it was a step toward world peace. But if SDI became a reality, it would pose the same problem that the antiballistic missiles had in the past: it would upset the balance of power. To the Soviets, Reagan was looking for a way to end the Cold War—but with a decisive victory for America. Arms talks stalled, and both sides continued to stockpile weapons.

Perhaps the most harmful blow to U.S.–Soviet relations came in the summer of 1983 when the Soviets shot down a South Korean airliner en route from New York to Seoul. The plane had flown off course and wandered into Soviet airspace. A Soviet pilot fired a missile, and the airliner went down; all 269 people aboard were killed. The Soviets claimed that the Korean plane had been used for reconnaissance, but few people believed them. The United States and its allies were outraged by the incident. Relations between East and West were at an all-time low, but change was on the way. A new Soviet leader, Mikhail Gorbachev, would be the force behind it.

In March of 1985 Communist officials elected Gorbachev as the new Soviet secretary-general, the leader of the Communist Party. Gorbachev recognized it was a time of "profound transformations." The people of his nation deserved a higher standard of living, he said, and he talked about reform—perestroika, or restructuring of the Soviet system. Perestroika would allow the Soviet people more involvement in decision making and would create a more open economy, so that citizens could earn profit from their work. Under Gorbachev's leadership, people eventually would be able to own farms and businesses; the government would not control all forms of commerce. Gorbachev also talked about glasnost, which means "openness."

"Frank information," he said, "is evidence of confidence in the people and respect for their intelligence and feelings, and for their ability to understand events for themselves." He believed there should be more candor and honest discussion about political and cultural activities in the Soviet Union. Newspapers, he said, should have more freedom to print what they chose, not what was supplied by the Communist Party. Young people should be able to listen to the music they wanted, even if it came from the West. Artists and writers should be able to create their work without fear of punishment, even if their creations were controversial. People should be able to voice their opinions without fear of arrest. Gorbachev would be the catalyst that ended the Cold War.

A Russian cartoon depicts the Soviet symbol of a hammer and sickle hatching from an egg labeled *perestroika* ("restructuring"). The suggestion seems to be that Russia's communist system will be reborn through reform.

Reagan's Star Wars Speech

As Reagan proposed the Star Wars project, many people questioned whether it was realistic—or even sane. It would be enormously expensive, and the technology hadn't reached the point where it was possible. Most scientists believed that even if it could be achieved, an enemy could figure out a way to overcome it. But these were not the only problems with the Star Wars program. If such a shield could be devised, the Soviets would no longer pose a threat. It would mean the end of mutual assured destruction, and the United States could launch a nuclear attack at any time. People all over the world, including Americans and the nation's allies, were critical of the plan. Even so, it would remain a goal for Reagan throughout his presidency, placing improved relations with the Soviets at risk. Following is a portion of the speech he gave introducing the Star Wars program to the public.

WE'RE ENGAGED RIGHT NOW in several negotiations with the Soviet Union to bring about a mutual reduction of weapons. . . . If the Soviet Union will join with us in our effort to achieve major arms reduction, we will have succeeded in stabilizing the nuclear balance. Nevertheless, it will still be necessary to rely on the specter of retaliation, on mutual threat. And that's a sad commentary on the human condition. Wouldn't it be better to save lives than to avenge them? Are we not capable of demonstrating our peaceful intentions by applying all our abilities and our ingenuity to achieving a truly lasting stability? I think we are. Indeed, we must. . . .

What if free people could live secure in the knowledge that their security did not rest upon the threat of instant U.S. retaliation to deter a Soviet attack, that we could intercept and destroy strategic ballistic missiles before they reached our own soil or that of our allies? . . .

I clearly recognize that defensive systems have limitations and raise certain problems and ambiguities. If paired with offensive systems, they can be viewed as fostering an aggressive policy, and no one wants that. But with these considerations firmly in mind, I call upon the scientific community in our country, those who gave us nuclear weapons, to turn their great talents now to the cause of mankind and world peace, to give us the means of rendering these nuclear weapons impotent and obsolete. . . .

"What if . . . we could intercept and destroy strategic ballistic missiles before they reached our own soil?"

I am directing a comprehensive and intensive effort to define a long-term research and development program to begin to achieve our ultimate goal of eliminating the threat posed by strategic nuclear missiles. This could pave the way for arms control measures to eliminate the weapons themselves. We seek neither military superiority nor political advantage. Our only purpose—one all people share—is to search for ways to reduce the danger of nuclear war.

—*From Ronald Reagan's "Address to the Nation on Defense and National Security," March 23, 1983.* The Public Papers of President Ronald W. Reagan, *Ronald Reagan Presidential Foundation and Library, Simi Valley, California.*

THINK ABOUT THIS

1. According to Reagan, why was SDI a better option than deterrence?

2. How could SDI make nuclear weapons "impotent and obsolete"?

3. Would you have supported Reagan's plans for SDI? Why or why not?

A Public Radio Report: The Superpowers Meet

Mikhail Gorbachev was a very different kind of Soviet leader. Young and energetic, he wanted to find a way to recharge the Soviet economy and to help the people of his nation. Gorbachev knew that to achieve the necessary changes, the USSR had to make drastic cuts in defense spending. He recognized the need to compromise with the West to find a way to stop the arms race and end the Cold War. Reagan liked what he heard about Gorbachev, and the two men agreed to meet in 1985. At the Geneva summit, the two men did not come to any major agreements, but they did forge a friendship that would lead to future breakthroughs in U.S.–Soviet relations. It was the beginning of the end of the Cold War. Following is an excerpt from a discussion between National Public Radio announcer Scott Simon and news analyst Daniel Schorr, who attended the summit.

Simon: Dan, you spent the entire week in Geneva. . . . Do you know of any other private moments that can be related now which you found out about through your sources in the sessions between the two [Gorbachev and Reagan]? Is the State Department convinced that Mr. Gorbachev represents a new regime and a new chance to deal with the Soviet Union?

Schorr: Yes, and so [is] President Reagan. President Reagan was actually rather taken by Gorbachev. . . . The fact of the matter is that Reagan came out and said something that I think is rather remarkable, considering the way he talked of Soviet lying and cheating all these years . . . he talked about Gorbachev as being, "Well, he's a

Communist all right, but I've decided he's very sincere." And I think that really marks the beginning of some kind of relationship.

Simon: The charm that has been reported about Mr. Gorbachev . . . seems to have affected Mr. Reagan. I'm wondering if you have any reading as to how our own president's charm seemed to ingratiate itself with the Soviet leader.

Schorr: To be frank, that's harder to tell because you don't get the kind of briefings from the Soviet side that the American delegation will give you. . . . I have the impression, but less clearly than you can get Reagan's impression, that Gorbachev came out feeling kind of like [Reagan's] a nice man but not a heavyweight.

Simon: I'm still impressed by the fact that Mr. Gorbachev held all these press conferences, that he met with [African-American politician] Jesse Jackson in a forty-five-minute session, and that he actually broached the question of his treatment of Soviet Jews. [The Soviets were often criticized for not allowing Jews to emigrate.] I'm assuming that none of that was for television back in the Soviet Union.

Schorr: Oh, yes, twenty minutes of the forty-five-minute meeting with Jesse Jackson was on Soviet television. Because no matter what else happens, they would like to tell people back there that there's not only Reagan in this country, but there is a peace opposition in this country. That remains very important from the point of view of their ideology.

Simon: Here's the question I've been preparing all week. Does our world become a safer place now that the two men have met and managed to get on with each other?

Schorr: Marginally, yes . . . there was not a single agreement on anything of any substance. They did not get anywhere on so-called Star Wars or anything else. It becomes marginally better because Reagan comes back and no longer talks about lying and cheating, but thinks he

"President Reagan was actually rather taken by Gorbachev."

understands that there is a man back there who heads a country with a different point of view, and they have somehow got to find ways to come to terms. They are doomed, as you might say, to coexist.

—From Weekend Edition, *Saturday November 23, 1985. In Linda Wertheimer, editor,* Listening to America: Twenty-five Years in the Life of a Nation as Heard on National Public Radio. *New York: Houghton Mifflin Company, 1995.*

THINK ABOUT THIS

1. According to Schorr, what positive steps were taken at the Geneva summit?

2. What surprised Simon about Gorbachev's actions during the summit?

3. According to Schorr, why did the Soviets agree to televise portions of the summit to their people?

Negotiation Breakdown: Gorbachev on the Reykjavík Summit

The superpowers came together for a second summit in Reykjavík, Iceland, in October 1986. Reagan assumed this would be another preliminary meeting, but what happened was quite different. Gorbachev was ready for serious negotiation. He proposed a 50 percent cut in all strategic arms and several other sweeping changes, including talks on a total ban on nuclear weapons testing. Not to be outdone, Reagan made an even more striking counterproposal: the elimination of all strategic missiles. The negotiations continued until the two sides decided to eliminate *all* nuclear weapons by 1996. But everything fell apart when Reagan refused to limit his SDI project. The meeting that seemed so promising ended in bitterness. What was the purpose of Star Wars, asked Gorbachev, if there were no missiles to shoot down? In the following excerpt, Gorbachev offers his view of events at the summit.

WE BROUGHT HERE A WHOLE PACKAGE of major proposals which, had they been accepted, could genuinely within a short period of time make it possible to . . . avert the threat of nuclear war and would also make it possible to begin movement toward a non-nuclear world. . . .

In the end, we made that last step. We said, in Europe, we will eliminate U.S. and Soviet medium-range missiles. In Asia, 100 warheads on missiles each. We agreed that an agreement to that effect could be signed.

In this situation, when we are entering the stage of genuine cuts, [we proposed] that in 10 years the nuclear arsenals of the Soviet Union and the United States would be eliminated altogether. . . .

We know the commitment of the U.S. Administration and the President to SDI. Our agreement to the possibility of lab testing makes possible for the President to go through with the research. . . . And this is really where the real fight began. The President insisted until the end that the United States retained the right

Edward Teller *(left)*, a physicist who worked on the Manhattan Project and is known as the "father of the H-bomb," applauds Reagan during a speech the president gave in 1988 in support of Star Wars. Teller played a key role in U.S. defense and energy policies for more than half a century and helped shaped Reagan's belief in a strong national defense.

to test, have experiments and to test things related to SDI not only in the laboratories but also out of the laboratories, including in space.

I said to the president that we were missing a historic chance. Never had our positions been so close together. When we were saying goodbye, the President said he was disappointed and that from the very beginning I, that is to say Gorbachev, had come to Reykjavík with no willingness to reach agreement. Why, he said, because of just one word are you so intransigent in your approach . . . ?

". . . we were missing a historic chance."

intransigent
immovable

No, it's not one word that is the point here. It is the substance that is the key to what the Administration really intends. If you make an inventory of things that have happened, you will see that we have made very serious, unprecedented concessions and compromises. . . . And still there has been no agreement. The Americans came to this meeting empty-handed, with an entire set of mothballed proposals.

*—From Mikhail Gorbachev's statement in Reykjavík, October 12, 1986.
In Edward J. Judge and John W. Langdon, editors,* The Cold War: A History
through Documents. *Upper Saddle River, NJ: Prentice Hall, 1996.*

THINK ABOUT THIS

Who do you think was right in this difference of opinion, Reagan or Gorbachev?

"Tear Down This Wall": Reagan in Berlin

Although Reykjavík seemed like a failure at the time, it did not slow the pace of change in the Soviet Union or curb Gorbachev's resolve to end the Cold War. Reagan saw and admired this. During a trip to Europe in 1987, he visited the city of Berlin—the longtime focus of

Cold War tensions. In a dramatic speech given in the shadow of the Berlin Wall, Reagan challenged Gorbachev to take reform a step further. Although he spoke in West Berlin, his words could be heard on the east side of the Wall. Following is an excerpt from that speech.

BEHIND ME STANDS A WALL that encircles the free sectors of this city, part of a vast system of barriers that divides the entire continent of Europe. From the Baltic, south, those barriers cut across Germany in a gash of barbed wire, concrete, dog runs, and guard towers. Farther south, there may be no visible, no obvious wall. But there remain armed guards and checkpoints all the same—still a restriction on the right to travel, still an instrument to impose upon ordinary men and women the will of a totalitarian state. . . .

[I]n the West today, we see a free world that has achieved a level of prosperity and well-being unprecedented in all human history. In the Communist world, we see failure, technological backwardness, declining standards of health, even want of the most basic kind—too little food. Even today, the Soviet Union still cannot feed itself. After these four decades, then, there stands before the entire world one great and inescapable conclusion: Freedom leads to prosperity. Freedom replaces the ancient hatreds among the nations with comity and peace. Freedom is the victor.

And now the Soviets themselves may, in a limited way, be coming to understand the importance of freedom. We hear much from Moscow about a new policy of reform and openness. Some political prisoners have been released. Certain foreign news broadcasts are no longer being jammed. Some economic enterprises have been permitted to operate with greater freedom from state control.

Are these the beginnings of profound changes in the Soviet state? Or are they token gestures, intended to raise false hopes in the West, or to strengthen the Soviet system without changing it? We welcome change and openness; for we believe that freedom and security go together, that the advance of human liberty can only strengthen the cause of world peace. There is one sign the Soviets can make that would be unmistakable, that would advance dramatically the cause of freedom and peace.

General Secretary Gorbachev, if you seek peace, if you seek prosperity for the Soviet Union and Eastern Europe, if you seek liberalization: Come here to this gate! Mr. Gorbachev, open this gate! Mr. Gorbachev, tear down this wall!

—From Ronald Reagan's "Remarks at the Brandenburg Gate," West Berlin, Germany, June 12, 1987. The Public Papers of President Ronald W. Reagan, *Ronald Reagan Presidential Foundation and Library, Simi Valley, California.*

THINK ABOUT THIS

1. According to Reagan, what factors indicated that the communist system did not work?

2. How, in Reagan's view, do "freedom and security go together"?

A Journalist Remembers: Dan Rather at the Wall

After Reykjavík, many believed there could be no hope for an arms agreement between the superpowers until a new U.S. president came into office. Gorbachev, however, decided that in spite of the U.S. position on SDI, he was ready to limit nuclear arms. He was, he said, prepared to sign a treaty to eliminate intermediate-range missiles in Europe. Reagan proposed that they eliminate *all* such missiles, including those based in Asia. With the signing of the INF (Intermediate-range Nuclear Forces) Treaty in 1987, the superpowers agreed to

The Berlin Wall, November 1989. For many, November 9, 1989—the day the East Germans finally "tore down the wall"—marked a symbolic end to the Cold War.

abolish a whole class of weapons. It was a first step toward the Treaty on the Reduction and Limitation of Strategic Offensive Arms, which Gorbachev and President George Bush would sign four years later. In April 1988 the Soviet Union finally agreed to pull its troops out of Afghanistan. Perhaps most remarkable of all, the Soviet Union released its grip on Eastern Europe. In an address to the United Nations, Gorbachev said that all nations must have the freedom to choose their own destiny. His words would have a powerful impact on the Soviet bloc. Free elections and new political parties appeared as the people of Eastern Europe began to determine their future independent of Soviet domination.

Some say it was NATO's London Declaration on July 6, 1990, that officially ended the Cold War. Proclaiming an end to the forty-six year struggle, it stated, "The Soviet Union has embarked on the long journey toward a free society. Europeans are determining their own destiny. They are choosing freedom." But for many people, the

Cold War ended the year before, on November 9, 1989, when the new East German government lifted all restrictions on travel between East and West Germany. As the day unfolded, joyful crowds of Berliners began to dismantle the Berlin Wall. Soon, in every country of the Soviet bloc in Eastern Europe, people rose up to oust the Communist regimes. A powerful force—the will of the people—had raised the Iron Curtain. Following is American television journalist Dan Rather's account of what happened that November, as the Wall came tumbling down.

STRANGE THINGS BEGAN HAPPENING around the Wall and inside Berlin itself. Pictures started rolling of people from East Germany actually crawling over the Wall. In the past, people making such attempts had been shot. This raised the question, where were the East German guards? If they were still at their posts, how were the defectors getting past them? A trickle can turn quickly into a stream, and rumors flashed across East and West Berlin that something was happening at the Wall. People began to gather on both sides of the Wall—not yet to celebrate but lured by curiosity as much as anything else.

The Wall was not down, but it was beginning to totter.

After the newscast one night, Tom Bettag [the producer of Rather's news program] and I caught the next plane for Berlin. . . .

The trickle of defectors had indeed turned into a stream. It was growing more obvious by the minute that the Wall was coming down, emotionally if not literally. No part of the Wall had been torn down physically, and while that was more than a formality, it was clearly a matter of time.

. . . the music that led into the broadcast was Beethoven—the "Ode to Joy" from the Ninth Symphony. "Joy" is an overused and overworked word, and we're lucky to feel the real thing six or seven times in our lives, but this was one occasion I thought the word was apt. The music soared like a skyburst of fireworks and rockets, and it was nothing compared to what the Germans were feeling that night.

. . . The next day I wanted to get up on the Wall itself, and so I did. . . . I just wanted to share what I saw happening all around me. The Wall was filled with Germans, East and West, some drinking champagne, some weeping, some laughing almost uncontrollably, hugging, singing, even engaging the East German border guards in conversation. People reached down to help others climb the Wall. . . .

I turned and saw that I had perched myself beside a German woman with two children. . . .

I said, simply, "What do you think?"

She clenched her fists and said, "My heart has exploded."

Her eyes glimmered, and I said, "That's really beautiful."

Then she hardened around the triangle of her eyes and nose. "The Russians will soon be gone," she said, and with a look that was icy, added, "and I can't wait for the rest of you to be gone."

I must have looked like someone who had been hit with a sledgehammer. She went on, "I don't dislike Americans, much less hate them as I hate the Russians. But you Americans don't know what it is to have foreigners occupy your soil, your fatherland." And we just looked at each other, until she turned her gaze once again across the expanse of concrete outside the Brandenburg Gate and into East Germany.

—*From Dan Rather and Mickey Herskowitz,* The Camera Never Blinks Twice: The Further Adventures of a Television Journalist. *New York: William Morrow and Company, 1994, pp. 170–173.*

THINK ABOUT THIS

1. Why was the fall of the Berlin Wall such an important moment in the Cold War?

2. Why was the German woman so anxious to have not only the Russians but all other non-Germans leave the country?

Time Line

1948

FEBRUARY 25: *Communist leaders take over Czechoslovakia.*

JUNE 24: *The Soviets begin the blockade of West Berlin.*

JUNE 26: *Airlift—U.S. and British forces begin flying supplies into West Berlin.*

AUGUST 3: *Whittaker Chambers accuses Alger Hiss of Communist activities.*

1946

FEBRUARY 22: *George Kennan's "Long Telegram" explains the Soviet threat.*

MARCH 5: *Churchill gives his "Iron Curtain" speech.*

1 9 4 0 s

1947

MARCH 12: *The Truman Doctrine: Truman asks Congress to aid Greece and Turkey in removing Communist rebels.*

JUNE 5: *The Marshall Plan: Secretary of State George Marshall announces the European Recovery Program.*

1945

APRIL 25: *Russian and American troops meet for the first time.*

MAY 7: *Germany officially surrenders.*

JULY 17–AUGUST 2: *The Potsdam Conference takes place.*

AUGUST 6: *The United States drops an atomic bomb on Hiroshima.*

AUGUST 9: *The United States drops a second bomb on Japan, this time on Nagasaki.*

AUGUST 10: *Japan surrenders.*

AUGUST 26: *The United States and the Soviet Union occupy Korea.*

APRIL 4: *NATO is established.*

MAY 12: *The blockade of West Berlin ends.*

AUGUST 29: *The Soviet Union successfully detonates an atomic bomb.*

OCTOBER 1: *The People's Republic of China is founded.*

1949

I LIKE IKE

1950

JANUARY 21: *Alger Hiss is convicted of perjury.*

FEBRUARY 20: *Joseph McCarthy delivers a speech to the Senate claiming to have a list of known Communists in the State Department.*

JUNE 25: *North Korea invades South Korea.*

NOVEMBER 1: *The United States detonates the first hydrogen bomb.*

1952

you can protect yourself from...

RADIOACTIVE FALLOUT

CD

GET THE FACTS!
FROM YOUR CIVIL DEFENSE DIRECTOR

FREE COURSE ON FALLOUT

place   date   time

1 9 5 0 s

JULY 26: *Fidel Castro officially begins the revolution in Cuba.*

JULY 27: *The Korean War ends.*

1953

JUNE 15: *United States stages first nationwide civil defense exercise.*

1955

JANUARY 12: *John Foster Dulles announces the strategy of "massive retaliation."*

DECEMBER 2: *The Senate condemns McCarthy, ending the McCarthy era.*

1954

JANUARY 1: *Castro assumes power in Cuba.*

1959

1961

APRIL 17: *The Bay of Pigs invasion fails in its attempt to "liberate" Cuba.*

AUGUST 13: *East Germany seals the border between East and West Berlin and starts building the Berlin Wall.*

1969

NOVEMBER 17: *Strategic Arms Limitation Talks (SALT) begin between the United States and USSR.*

1972

FEBRUARY 17–27: *Nixon visits the People's Republic of China.*

MAY 26: *Nixon and Brezhnev sign the SALT and ABM treaties.*

1973

JANUARY 23: *Nixon announces the Vietnam War will end in sixty days.*

JUNE 26: *Kennedy visits Berlin and declares, "Ich bin ein Berliner."*

AUGUST 5: *The Nuclear Test Ban Treaty is signed.*

1963

1975

AUGUST 1: *The Helsinki Final Act is signed.*

1 9 6 0 s   1 9 7 0 s

JULY 1: *The Nuclear Non-Proliferation Treaty is signed.*

1968

OCTOBER 16: *The People's Republic of China detonates its first nuclear bomb.*

1964

AUGUST 8: *Nixon resigns.*

MARCH 25: *Anti-Vietnam War rallies are staged in the United States and Europe.*

1966

1974

OCTOBER 14: *The Cuban Missile Crisis begins.*

1962

OCTOBER 28: *Khrushchev and Kennedy negotiate an end to the Cuban Missile Crisis.*

JUNE 18: *The SALT II agreement is signed.*

1979

DECEMBER 25: *The Red Army enters Afghanistan.*

1983

MARCH 23: *Reagan proposes the Strategic Defense Initiative ("Star Wars").*

SEPTEMBER 1: *A Soviet jet fighter shoots down a Korean passenger plane.*

MARCH 13: *Mikhail Gorbachev comes to power.*

NOVEMBER 19: *Reagan and Gorbachev meet for the first time at the Geneva summit.*

1985

SEPTEMBER–DECEMBER: *Eastern European nations leave the Soviet bloc.*

NOVEMBER 9: *The Berlin Wall falls.*

1989

JULY 6: *NATO's London Declaration officially ends the Cold War.*

1990

1 9 8 0 s   1 9 9 0 s

1991

JULY 31: *Bush and Gorbachev sign START treaty, pledging to destroy thousands of strategic nuclear weapons.*

DECEMBER 8: *Reagan and Gorbachev sign the INF Treaty.*

1987

OCTOBER 11–12: *The Gorbachev–Reagan arms talks at Reykjavík stall over Reagan's refusal to limit SDI research.*

1986

APRIL 14: *The Soviet Union agrees to withdraw its forces from Afghanistan.*

DECEMBER 7: *Gorbachev gives a speech to the United Nations promising freedom for nations in the Soviet bloc.*

1988

Glossary

capitalism an economic system in which private individuals or groups can own land, factories, and other means of production, using the hired labor of others to produce goods and services for profit

communiqué an official communication

communism an economic system in which most or all property is owned by the government

détente the relaxation of strained relations or tensions

deterrent a factor that acts to prevent something from happening

exile a person who is banished from his or her country

fallout the toxic particles that fall to the earth after a nuclear explosion

foreign policy the plan and management of a nation's dealings with other countries

guerrillas fighters who use surprise and stealth instead of direct combat to wear down a better-equipped enemy

ideology the ideas, theories, and aims that make up a person's or group's core beliefs

leftist organizations political groups who aim to reform or overthrow the established order in the hope of helping common people

munitions military supplies used in war, such as guns, tanks, and bombs

oppression cruel or unjust treatment by an authority

paramilitary troops that are trained to act like an official military force

proletariat the laboring class; people in a community who do not have the means to produce goods on their own and who thus sell their labor to live

reconnaissance a military mission, often secretive, to gain information about the enemy

socialism an economic system that stresses public or community ownership of farms, factories, and other property as opposed to private ownership

subversive something that acts secretly to overthrow or undermine a government or political system

totalitarian regime a government that takes away the rights of the individual by maintaining control of all aspects of life

To Find Out More

BOOKS

Collier, Christopher, and James Lincoln Collier. *The United States in the Cold War 1945– 1989* (Drama of American History series). New York: Benchmark Books, 2001.

Gorbachev, Mikhail Sergeyevich. *Gorbachev: On My Country and the World.* Translated by George Shriver. New York: Columbia University Press, 1999.

Isaacs, Jeremy, and Taylor Downing. *Cold War: An Illustrated History, 1945–1991.* Boston: Little, Brown & Company, 1998.

Kennedy, Robert F. *Thirteen Days: A Memoir of the Cuban Missile Crisis.* New York: W. W. Norton & Company, 1969.

Matthews, John R. *The Rise and Fall of the Soviet Union* (World History series). San Diego, CA: Lucent Books, 2000.

Rice, Earle. *The Cold War: Collapse of Communism* (History's Great Defeats series). San Diego, CA: Lucent Books, 2000.

Ruggiero, Adriane. *American Voices from World War II.* New York: Benchmark Books, 2003.

Schomp, Virginia. *American Voices from the Vietnam Era.* New York: Benchmark Books, 2004.

Sherrow, Victoria. *Joseph McCarthy and the Cold War* (Notorious Americans and Their Times series). Woodbridge, CT: Blackbirch, 1998.

Smith, Samantha. *Journey to the Soviet Union.* Boston: Little, Brown & Company, 1985.

Streissguth, Thomas. *Life in Communist Russia* (The Way People Live series). San Diego, CA: Lucent Books, 2001.

Vail, John J. *"Peace, Land, Bread!": A History of the Russian Revolution* (World History Library). New York: Facts on File, 1996.

Winkler, Allan M. *The Cold War: A History in Documents* (Pages from History series). New York: Oxford University Press Children's Books, 2001.

VIDEO

CNN Perspectives: Cold War. CNN Productions, Warner Home Video, 1998.

WEB SITES

The Web sites listed here were in existence in 2003–2004 when this book was being written. Their names or locations may have changed since then.

In general, when using the Internet to do research on a history topic, you should use caution. You will find numerous Web sites that are very attractive to look at and appear to be professional in format. Proceed with caution, however. Many, even the best ones, contain errors. Some Web sites even insert disclaimers or warnings about mistakes that may have made their way into the site. In the case of primary sources, the builders of the Web site often transcribe previously published material, good or bad, accurate or inaccurate. Therefore, you have to judge the content of *all* Web sites. This requires a critical eye.

A good rule for using the Internet as a resource is always to compare what you find in Web sites to several other sources such as librarian- or teacher-recommended reference works and major works of scholarship. By doing this, you will discover the myriad versions of history that exist.

http://www.cnn.com/SPECIALS/cold.war/ is the companion Web site to the acclaimed CNN television series on the Cold War.

http://www.civildefensemuseum.com/, the Civil Defense Museum Web site, features radio spots, photos, posters, and more from the Cold War period.

http://www.gwu.edu/~nsarchiv/coldwar/documents/, the Web site of the National Security Archive, is an excellent resource for primary sources from the Cold War era, including many declassified top-secret documents from the U.S. government.

http://www.nuclearfiles.org/hitimeline/index.html provides a fascinating time line of the nuclear age, sponsored by the Nuclear Age Peace Foundation.

http://cwihp.si.edu/ is the Web site of the Cold War International History Project, sponsored by the Woodrow Wilson International Center for Scholars. It features primary sources from around the world.

http://www.spymuseum.org/index.asp is the Web site of the International Spy Museum, an excellent page to learn more about espionage during the Cold War.

The presidential libraries are excellent resources for primary source documents and photographs. Visit the following libraries for information about the Cold War:

The Truman library:
http://www.trumanlibrary.org/

The Dwight D. Eisenhower Library and Museum:
http://www.eisenhower.utexas.edu/

The Kennedy Library:
http://www.cs.umb.edu/jfklibrary/

The Lyndon Baines Johnson Library and Museum:
http://www.lbjlib.utexas.edu/

The Nixon Foundation:
http://www.nixonfoundation.org/

Gerald R. Ford Library and Museum:
http://www.ford.utexas.edu/

Jimmy Carter Library and Museum:
http://www.jimmycarterlibrary.org/

Ronald Reagan Presidential Library:
http://www.reagan.utexas.edu/

Index

Page numbers for illustrations are in boldface

ABOUT THE AUTHOR

Elizabeth Sirimarco published her first book in 1990. Since that time she has written books for young people on subjects ranging from tennis to Thomas Jefferson, the Yanomami to Steven Spielberg. "The best thing about writing," she says, "is that I still have the chance to learn new things—it's like being in school again. Kids probably wouldn't understand—I wouldn't have believed it at their age—but I really miss school!"

A graduate of the University of Colorado at Boulder, Elizabeth also earned a degree in Italian from the Università per Stranieri in Siena, Italy. In addition to writing, she is an editor and occasionally enjoys the opportunity to work as an Italian translator. She and her husband, David, a photographer, live with their rottweiler and two cats in Denver, Colorado.